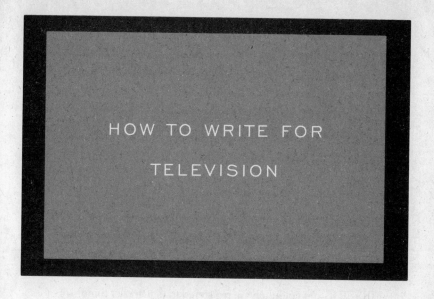

HOW TO WRITE FOR TELEVISION

Madeline DiMaggio

A Fireside Book
Published by Simon & Schuster
New York   London   Toronto   Sydney

Fireside
A Division of Simon & Schuster, Inc.
1230 Avenue of the Americas
New York, NY 10021

This Fireside trade paperback edition November 2008

FIRESIDE and colophon are registered trademarks of Simon
& Schuster, Inc.

For information about special discounts for bulk purchases,
please contact Simon & Schuster Special Sales at 1-800-456-6798
or business@simonandschuster.com.

Designed by Mary Austin Speaker

Manufactured in the United States of America

10 9 8 7 6 5 4 3 2 1

Library of Congress Cataloging-in-Publication Data
DiMaggio, Madeline
     How to write for television / Madeline DiMaggio.
        p. cm.
     1. Television authorship. 2. Television plays—Technique.
  I. Title.
  PN1992.7.D5   1990
  808'.066791—dc20   89-37579
                                                CIP

ISBN-13: 978-1-4165-7045-5
ISBN-10:   1-4165-7045-4

To my mother and silent partner, Mary Marsh DiMaggio;
To my daughter, Jordan, my greatest accomplishment;
And to Joyce Barkley, who put the whole thing in motion

CONTENTS

I.

INTRODUCTION

TV IS WHERE IT'S HAPPENING. It's where the money is, where the jobs are, where product is pumped out fast, and where writers have the privilege of seeing their material produced. This isn't necessarily so in films, where the process is very slow and the writer can be a one-hit wonder.

According to Writers Guild of America statistics, TV jobs outnumber film jobs by two to one. There are about four hundred movies made a year, and about three thousand television episodes. In television, if writers can find a way in, if they have the talent and know how to play it, they can go from a freelancer to a staff position, to story editor, to producer/creator, and even rise to the pinnacle of television, the showrunner. It happens; one of my former students even managed to pick up four Emmys along the way. And there are others who have achieved success. They have wonderful stories, some of which I will share with you.

I don't take credit for their success. It doesn't validate me as a teacher: they had what it takes. But their success validates what I believe in—that achieving dreams does happen.

The business of television has changed since this book was first written, and I have changed as well. I continue to write, and I have sold movies to cable and television and sold two feature films. I'm currently attached to numerous projects, have a number of screenplays under option, and continue to teach. My screenwriting workshops have taken me to colleges and universities across the country, and farther. I've taught soap writing in Finland, where conflict is considered disrespectful (try that one!), and sitcom writing to the Chinese who don't speak a word of English (that one's even better!). My favorite workshops are the small private ones, where I work with writers in helping them develop their scripts. Getting to know my students and watching them grow as writers has made teaching a very satisfying part of my life.

Many of these writers are on their fifth and sixth screenplays. They get better with each script. If I see a project I think has market appeal, I will try with all my power to help them find access.

Two years ago I joined forces with another writer/producer, Joanne Storkan, and we formed the banner Honest Engine Films. I see the market from a different perspective now—from both the buyer's and seller's point of view. I've become one of those people who too often says, "I'm sorry, we have to pass." I hate saying those words, because I know how the writer feels on the other end. But producing has given me many new insights, which I have shared with my students and will share with you throughout this book.

I make no false promises about this business. Let's face it: deciding to make a living by writing television scripts is not often a practical or easy career choice.

Television agent Mitch Stein, whom I interview later in the book, told me that when he speaks at conferences he likes to sit at the end of the dais, so when they finally get to him and ask his advice, he can tell everybody in the room, "Go buy a bus ticket and get out of town. Someday you will thank me for it."

Consider this:

The Writers Guild of America, West, and Writers Guild of America, East, together represent about 11,000 members, about half of whom work in a given year. According to Chuck Slocum, Assistant Executive Director who tracks all the numbers for both Guilds, out of the working half of the membership, the median income from writing over a five-year period is $62,000 per year.

There are about 3,000 episodes of television written each year. Almost all of them are written by staff writers. On average a series has about a dozen writers. Now for the good news.

It can be done—you *can* break into television writing. It happened to me; it's happened to some of my students. The industry is full of writers who somehow managed to buck the odds. Not all of these writers are related to somebody, nor did they all begin with contacts. Some of them lived outside the LA area. Their stories are as diverse as their personalities and the TV shows they write for. But the writers did all have one thing in common—good ideas, well-written spec scripts, and some knowledge of marketing. The spec scripts were their calling card. They opened doors to an eventual sale.

THE STORY OF KEVIN FALLS

I met Kevin in Los Altos, California, at Foothill College. It was one of my first college classes. He was a journalism major from Cal Poly. He had wonderful energy and enthusiasm and didn't miss a beat. I read his first screenplay; it was quite good, and I could tell that he had talent. The script didn't sell, but in the marketing process, Kevin found an agent. He kept writing. He completed his second screenplay—it also didn't sell—but he kept writing. One day I got a call from him. He was angry and distraught. He had three completed screenplays to his credit and still no bites. I completely understood his frustration, but I had a feeling he wouldn't give up.

About six months later I heard from him again. He called to tell me he had just signed a four-picture deal with Disney Studios. An executive there, a woman whom I came to know later, had read one of his scripts. She was not interested in buying the script, but she loved the way it was written. She called Kevin's agent and asked to read more. The agent sent down those two other scripts that had never sold. Again, for various reasons, she didn't buy the scripts, but she found the writing wonderful. It was not only consistent, but Kevin's style was perfect for the Disney genre. He was immediately placed under contract.

I saw Kevin a number of years later at a writer's conference in Hawaii where I was speaking with Kathie Fong Yoneda, a former executive at Disney Studios.

Kevin, at the time, had just signed on to write the *Pretty Woman* sequel, a project that later was shelved because of casting problems, and he, at the moment, was writing the movie *The Temp*. During the Q & A, a young hopeful asked Kevin how many spec scripts he had written before he sold one. Kevin responded, "Seven." The kid's mouth dropped open. He asked what kept him going, and I'll never forget Kevin's answer. He said he was getting on the Bayshore freeway, and asked himself the same thing, *What if I never sell a screenplay?* And he got the answer. *It doesn't matter. I'll just leave them to my kids. I love it so much I'm going to keep on writing anyway.*

I kept track of Kevin's career because his name kept popping up on the television screen, and I saw him year after year picking up Emmys.

We met for a drink when I asked to interview him for my book. At the time his new show, *Journeyman*, was on the air. It was a great series, intelligently written, intricately woven, and filled with whopper surprises, but the timing was bad: the writers' strike was about to hit just as the show was gaining momentum, and *Journeyman*, along with some other good series, would become one of its casualties.

Kevin's enthusiasm hadn't waned. It was pretty clear he still loved what he did. I asked him when he had made the turn from features to television. He said he was a big sports fan, and when he heard HBO was doing *Arli$$*, a show about a sports agent, he looked into it and got on staff. He stayed with the show for three years, then wanted off. His agent convinced him to hang on for one more year and he'd get him a co-executive producer credit, and that would later help him get a better network job. A year passed, and the agent asked Kevin where he wanted to go. Kevin was a huge fan of *Sports Night*. When he heard they were looking for somebody, he got a knot in his stomach; he'd give anything just to be in the same room with those people. He met with the staff twice and didn't think it went well. But at the third meeting, Aaron Sorkin was there and asked Kevin if he could start that day—at noon. He said it was the single most fulfilling moment of his career to be a co-executive producer with Aaron Sorkin on *Sports Night*! He continued working with Sorkin on *The West Wing*, where he served as co-executive producer for sixty-seven episodes that garnered four Emmys before going out on his own. Since then, he's been executive producer, creator, and showrunner for shows too numerous to mention. Go to imdb.com and type in his name if you'd like to see a list of his credits: it's two pages long.

My friend Pamela Wallace (Academy Award winner for *Witness*) believes that there's a defining moment in every character's life that subconsciously designs who they will become. I think that happens in our professional lives as well. For Kevin, I think it happened the day he was driving down the street and asked himself what he would do if he never sold a screenplay. He decided it didn't matter; he was going to keep writing anyway. I think that was the moment that defined Kevin Falls's success.

There are two ways you can learn to write for television. One is to read television scripts, and the other is to write them. "How to" books are helpful, and I certainly hope you buy this one. But when you get right down to it, there is no text better than the actual script. For this reason, I have included in this book excerpts of scripts I have collaborated on or written in half-hour, one-hour, and two-hour movie formats. I use these examples to facilitate stepping you through the development process. They make it easier, because you have actual pages of action, narrative, and dialogue in front of you.

We will begin with the basic tenets of scriptwriting, then move on to the hooks that television rests on. We'll analyze these hooks so you'll know what producers are looking for in spec scripts. My goal is that you'll never watch the tube the same way again—that every time you turn on your television set, you'll recognize what we've discussed, and your education will become much more than a one-time read.

Once we've studied the mechanics of scriptwriting and the tenets on which television rests, we will move into structure. Together, we will go through the necessary steps in developing scripts for the three formats.

Books on television, for the most part, don't cover writing the two-hour movie. I feel it's extremely important from a marketing standpoint for new writers to have a spec feature, cable, or TV movie in their arsenal to market. I've spoken to agents and producers to get a consensus, and they agree. There are two reasons for this. The spec movie is a great sample of the writer's original voice, and it also can be marketed to cable companies by producers before the writer has credits, and even before he or she has an agent. In fact, sometimes it's the way to an agent. Writing a small movie and getting a producer attached is a great way for new writers to get access and get read.

Finally, we will cover marketing. What is the point of crafting something sensational unless you know how to get it out there and get it read?

In my lecturing and various workshops, I have found my best instruction comes through my personal experiences in the industry. These include the horror stories as well as the victories. I've made mistakes, and I am bluntly honest about them. I point out these errors to educate you. I don't have all the answers. For everything I tell you there will be exceptions. Everything in this business is subjective.

This book is intended to be a how-to, as well as a what-not-to-do for the industry. My intention is to instruct and to entertain. What's the point of all this work unless we can have a little fun along the way?

2.

THE TOOLS OF SCRIPTWRITING

WRITING FOR TELEVISION AND FILMS is an "art of less," the Zen of writing. Unlike the novel, the script is not complete; it is a series of visual impressions giving the illusion of completeness. Here, the writer's perception must shift from the words to the picture. The goal is to show, not to talk about, to indicate or to suggest rather than to explain. Since the scriptwriter is working within terrific time limitations (a half hour, one hour, or two hours), his or her purpose is to select the right fragments and pictures that most effectively tell the story, while eliminating all the excess fat.

When you read television scripts (teleplays) and film scripts—and it is absolutely essential that you read them—you will be amazed at how simple they appear. The simplicity is an illusion because a good script is so economical. Often the picture is enough. What scriptwriters choose to leave out is as important as what they choose to put in. Television and film writing is a visual art form; therefore, it requires more than just literary skills. A good visual sense is absolutely crucial. Timing and rhythm are also important, as well as an ability to resonate with the audience. Certainly, if you have no sense of what the viewing masses will like or identify with, your stories will not be marketable. Last, but certainly not least, you need a flair for the dramatic, because first and foremost, your job is to entertain.

Unlike the novelist, the scriptwriter has only three tools with which to work in moving the story forward. These are

Locales: Choosing the picture.
Narrative/Action: Describing what is taking place in
    the picture.
Dialogue: What is being said in the picture.

Together these tools combine and create the

Scene: The unit of action that moves the story forward,
    and the building block of the script.

LOCALES

Choosing Your Pictures

The locale is the place. It is the visual backdrop you use to tell your story. Since it is a place, it has an interior or exterior. In film and television, it also has a time. The time is either day or night.

Imagine yourself sitting in front of the TV set. You're watching *Grey's Anatomy*. In this particular episode, Dr. Erica Hawn has come to replace Dr. Burke at Seattle Grace, and it's her first day on the job. The locale is the nurses' station. Hawn stands with the Chief, who introduces her to Dr. Derek Shepherd and Dr. Mark Sloan. She comments snidely as they leave that they are "ridiculously attractive." Does the Chief hire on looks alone?

The location now shifts to the stairwell, where Derek and Mark talk about the Chief's crazy idea of a men's night out. What exactly is a men's night out? Will there be strippers involved?

The locale again changes. Now we are in the hospital corridor, where Derek passes Dr. Meredith Grey and Dr. Christina Yang. Derek and Meredith exchange casual hellos. Yang knows something is up. Meredith tells her they are meeting later for some breakup sex.

Once again the locale shifts, as doctors Callie Torres, Alex Karev, George O'Malley, and "Izzie" Stevens rush to the emergency entrance, where two ambulances are arriving.

Above are four different locations. Each location creates a new scene. They would appear in the script like this:

```
INT. MEDICAL STATION — DAY

INT. STAIRWELL — DAY

INT. HALLWAY — DAY

EXT. EMERGENCY — DAY
```

Every time a location changes, you are almost always watching the work of the writer. How the picture is shot and its different angles are always the work of the director. The scriptwriter creates the locale; the director decides how to shoot it.

Count how often locales change in a given one-hour episode and you will understand the medium of "moving" pictures.

The above four scenes in *Grey's Anatomy* ran three minutes! There was a time when one-hour shows rested on car chases and heavy action. Now, with ensemble casts and multiple storylines, the quick cuts and fast pace are what keep the action going.

Study the show you want to write for and it will dictate its location parameters. *Grey's Anatomy* keeps the majority of its action in the hospital. The set locales outside the hospital are Meredith and Izzie's apartment, the bar, and Derek's trailer. The show periodically takes us to other locales when needed. Locations are constrained by time and budgets. If you write a spec *Grey's Anatomy*, it is best to keep the locales "in house," meaning within the set locations the show regularly uses.

If you were writing a spec teleplay of *The Closer*, you would know that Deputy Police Chief Brenda Johnson runs a Priority Homicide Division of the LAPD. Each week, Chief Johnson is sent to a different location. Therefore, within budget rationale, you have most of LA to choose from as your palette of locales. In *CSI: Miami*, you have all of Miami; in *Women's Murder Club*, you have all of San Francisco. Even though you will want to keep the number of your locations down because of budgetary constraints, you can still make them interesting or provocative. Show us something fresh or something indigenous to the city; give us a backdrop that will fascinate us or educate us. We are all so tired of going to the same old places. Do some research: it's fun!

Locales do much more than present a background for action; they can create a mood and change the tone of a story. Let's suppose you are crafting a scene in which a man and a woman profess their love for each other. You decide the locale should be a steel mill, and they have to yell over the grinding industrial noise to communicate their feelings to each other. Take the same dialogue, and now imagine placing the lovers on the beach in Malibu. What you will have are two very different scenes, two very different moods. The visuals you choose hold the audience's interest; they create backdrops and influence the dialogue and the tone for that show.

Good scriptwriters use interesting and unique locales. They bring the very best visuals they can to a script because they understand the rule of film: that is, the viewer would rather watch than listen. When television audiences turn on the tube, what they want to see are pictures. If they only wanted words, they'd buy novels. Look around you and see your world as a filmmaker. Everywhere you look is a potential backdrop.

NARRATIVE/ACTION

Narrative describes what is taking place in the locale. It opens up the picture and describes all the action. In order to generate interest, a script must first be a good read, one in which the reader is compelled to turn the page. A good read is a visual read and good narrative makes the picture come alive. Narrative tells a story. If we equate choosing the locale to choosing the canvas, then we can equate writing the narrative to filling the canvas with a paintbrush. Every word in the narrative, every stroke matters.

In *MUFFON*, a sci-fi thriller I wrote, a disenfranchised aerospace engineer is blackballed for mental illness after reporting an abduction. The angry engineer finds five fellow abductees who share the same horrifying experience, and together they break into a top-secret facility to prove a government cover-up and clear their names.

I wanted the reader, in the opening of the script, to feel the sense of being trapped. I felt this would set the tone of the piece and convey the emotional state of my protagonist, John Coulter. I chose the locale of the Los Padres National Forest. I envisioned a condor soaring into view, the master of its world. Suddenly it's trapped by human hands. Next, I wanted to introduce my protagonist and see in his eyes the same sense of threat. I also wanted to have a little fun and play with a bit of humor that runs throughout the script.

```
EXT. LOS PADRES NATIONAL FOREST — DAY

A magnificent condor with an eight-foot wingspan soars
into view and glides to a perch high on a cliff. The
bird snaps to a heightened awareness. Suddenly, a net
descends upon it; tightens. We hear MUFFLED HUMAN
VOICES. Gloved hands come from nowhere, immobilizing it.
In the bird's eyes, absolute terror.


INT./EXT. A VINTAGE VOLVO — NIGHT

As it moves through a suburban neighborhood, the driver,
JOHN COULTER, checks an address. He's intense, mid to
late thirties, in great shape. A bit unkempt right now.
In his eyes, there's uncertainty—a heightened awareness
of threat—not unlike the condor's. He finds the modest
house. Parks, hesitates. A dog starts BARKING O.S.


EXT. THE MARTINEZ HOUSE

As he approaches, LIGHTS BLAST ON like a prison yard.
Coulter's momentarily blinded. These are no ordinary
```

```
lights; they are halogen arcs, triggered by the
slightest movement.


INT. MARTINEZ HOUSE — BEDROOM

JESSIE MARTINEZ, Hispanic, late twenties, watches the
scene outside from a security monitor. Entrances flash
"BOLTED." Infrared scanners BLINK "ON."
She grabs an AK-47, releases the safety.


EXT. MARTINEZ HOUSE — NIGHT

The CAMERA picks up Coulter tentatively approaching.
A NEIGHBOR yells from a parked car O.S. BLASTING THE
HORN.

                    NEIGHBOR
          Shut off the lights, Martinez! If I
          wanted a suntan I'd be in Aruba.


Coulter spots the barrel of an AK-47 emerge from a
window. POW! A shot pierces the air. The car horn stops.
The semiautomatic now turns on him.

                    MARTINEZ
          What do you want?

                    COULTER
          Maybe this is a bad time . . .
```

Like other elements in the script, narrative should be lean. Good painters know when to stop painting the canvas. They know where to leave spaces.

Some locales require more narrative than others. For example, if you are describing Star City, the Russian space facility that was a state secret until the late 1980s, more words will be needed, but all of us have been to a city bookstore or to a Starbucks.

Style of narrative writing varies greatly among writers. Read teleplays and screenplays and find a narrative style that really clicks for you, one with which you feel comfortable. Play with it; adapt it to yourself. Before long, you will discover that you are developing a narrative style that is all your own.

Writing good narrative is a challenge. The writer must always ask, What are the words that most descriptively or metaphorically get my message across? The wonderful thing about writers is that no two will ever choose the same thing.

DIALOGUE

Dialogue is a crucial and necessary element of all good scripts. Good dialogue reveals character and provides conflict. It works on two levels—the spoken and the unspoken. It provides exposition, communicating facts and advancing the plot. Good dialogue is economical, but is it real? Not really. It's much leaner; it gives the illusion of being real. Try taping a normal conversation at your local IHOP and then transcribing it into script dialogue. It would be terribly overwritten. We all overtalk!

Like music, good dialogue has a natural pace and rhythm. It's a dance of short speeches that bounce back and forth.

How does good dialogue happen? It comes from knowing your character, because each character has his or her own voice.

House has a unique voice, so does Dexter, and Nicki on *Big Love*. The entire cast of *Friends* had unique voices. If you covered the characters' names on a script, you would still know for whom the dialogue was intended.

A character's voice comes from the person's perception and point of view on the world. It's created by their past and creates their present experience. No two characters have the same voice. Rachel Green in *Friends* grew within the context of the series, but she would always struggle with the spoiled, image-conscious Daddy's girl who fled from her wedding in the pilot show and found her way to Monica's apartment.

The success of a television show rests on characters such as these. They are someone else's creation. As TV writers choosing to write on spec, it is your job to know these shows, not to change them. And know them you must.

Dialogue works on two levels: what is being said, and its intended meaning, or subtext. As humans, we talk around subjects; we don't hit them on the head.

Acting classes come in especially handy for writing dialogue. I highly recommend them to all writers. I began my career as an actor, and I have used many acting exercises and applied them to my writing classes—using sense memory, subtext, and various other techniques to bring the writer into the present life and private moments of the character. We writers are so often busy with the hard work of writing, we stay outside the material, manipulating it rather than being inside it and feeling it. When we get inside our characters and our stories, that's when the great things happen.

Good dialogue is rewritten dialogue. A writer plays with it and tries it different ways. The first draft exists to be rewritten. The rewrite is where dialogue is honed and trimmed. It's like the diamond that exists within the rock: first the excess must be chipped away. Good dialogue is precise, economical, and mercilessly cut.

One of my favorite quotes on rewriting is by the late, great Paddy Chayefsky, Academy Award winner for the movie *Network*, who said, "My own rules are very simple. First, cut out all the wisdom. Then cut out all the adjectives. I've cut some of my favorite stuff. I have no compassion when it comes to cutting. No pity or sympathy."

I tell my writers, if all good writers were doctors, they'd be surgeons. All dialogue should move the action forward. Everything extraneous, all excess fat should go.

Dialogue and Plot Progression

A movie I spec-wrote entitled *Swing Sisters* is a music-driven drama loosely based on the International Sisters of Rhythm, the first female integrated band, who came together during WWII. The protagonist is Jeannie Jerome, a pianist and composer. Jeannie and her brother, Billy, grew up on the road with their single dad, who played jazz trumpet in clubs from New Orleans to Chicago.

In the scene below, Jeannie has searched everywhere for the right singer to front her band and sing her music. She finally hears the voice she has been looking for on a radio jingle and tells her agent to find the singer. She wants to hire her, sight unseen.

```
INT. JEANNIE'S BROWNSTONE — MORNING

Jeannie's at the piano. There's a knock at the door.
GLORIA REYNOLDS stands there. She's twenty-three,
sophisticated, beautiful, and black. Gloria wryly
smiles waiting for her reaction.
```

                    JEANNIE
          You must be Gloria.

                    GLORIA
          Surprised? You weren't expecting this.

Jeannie wasn't. She doesn't react, she holds out her
hand to Gloria instead.

                    JEANNIE
          I'm Jeannie Jerome.

                    GLORIA
          How does that offer stand now?

                    JEANNIE
           . . . It stands.

                    GLORIA
          So how's it supposed to work? We all
          pile into a bus, just me and all the
          white girls?

Jeannie's caught off guard by her brashness.

                    JEANNIE
          I don't have all my sidemen
          yet. . . . Look, my Dad played jazz
          in a black quintet . . . Scat Robbins
          taught me the piano. What I care about
          is how good you are.

                    GLORIA
          That's all fine that you grew up in
          the "black-and-tanners," and some
          Negro taught you how to play the
          piano, but at the end of the day it
          doesn't make you colorblind.

                    JEANNIE
          This is about my music. You either
          sing it, or you don't. Besides that,
          you don't know a damn thing about me.

Billy bolts out of the bedroom in uniform. He's carrying
a knapsack.

                         BILLY
              Goddamn, I'm late for the Port
              Authority! In twenty minutes I'm AWOL.
                         (he spots Gloria)
              Sorry, I didn't know Jeannie had
              company.
                         (backing out the door)
              I'll call when we land . . . the first
              shot I have at a phone.
                         (to Gloria)
              Didn't mean to interrupt, just go back
              to whatever it was you were doing. See
              ya.

And BAM! He's out the door. After a beat Gloria turns back.

                         GLORIA
              You have lead sheets?

AT THE PIANO

they share the bench. Gloria sings with Jeannie on
harmony. She plays some chords then takes over at the
piano. Jeannie's impressed. She joins her at the bridge.
Their voices blend beautifully.

                         GLORIA
              That's a great tune.

                         JEANNIE
              I've written a lot of them.

                         GLORIA
              Being Negro is gonna cause a whole lot
              of problems.

                         JEANNIE
              My music's more important.

                         GLORIA
              You said you needed sidemen. Are your
              auditions open?

It's another dare and Jeannie knows it, it carries with it
more consequences.

In the above scene, we have supplied pertinent information to move the story forward.

- Gloria, the secondary character in the story, is introduced. She is black and expecting not to get the job. She has attitude and can be difficult.
- Both she and Jeannie are pros at what they do, but there is obvious tension between them from the get-go.
- This is Gloria and Billy's first meeting. They later fall in love, which is the subplot of the story, and their love ultimately breaks up the band.
- The result of open auditions is black twins on bass and sax, and a Puerto Rican drummer. Jeannie's agent has a fit, but she tells him she won't settle for anything less than the best musicians she can find, and these ladies are it.

Dialogue and Subtext

In my early days of writing episodic television, producers and story editors would sometimes make a notation on the script: "too on the nose" or "fix it." I soon learned that the phrase "on the nose" meant the dialogue was too literal, too obvious.

Good dialogue happens on two levels: what is being said, and what is being implied, the subtext. We all talk around things; we don't hit them on the head. Subtext is the layer of dialogue where characters hide. It's where they camouflage their true intentions and feelings; it's the part of themselves they don't want seen or uncovered. As a writer you know your character's weak spots and it's your job to uncover them. Think of subtext as a game of hide-and-seek with your characters. Let them feel safe, allow them the cover-up, and then, in their most vulnerable moments let their true motives and feelings start to peek through. These vulnerable moments almost always happen through conflict. It's when we all let down our defenses.

The Swing Sisters fight amongst themselves, experience prejudice as a band, as women, and live the horrors of the Jim Crow laws while playing segregated military bases in the South. These struggles bring them closer, and Jeannie and Gloria forge a deep bond. When Jeannie discovers Gloria and her brother have been secretly seeing each other and are deeply in love, she is against the relationship. She's seen too much, and she says they're setting themselves for pain.

In the following scene, Gloria has walked out on the band. She tells Jeannie it was okay to have a Negro as her best friend, just not to have one in the family. Jeannie turns to her only ally, her boyfriend Mitch.

```
INT. MITCH'S APARTMENT — DAY

Jeannie sits on the sofa, her head in her hands.

                    JEANNIE
          I should have done more to stop them.

                    MITCH
          Like what? You can't control who you
          love. It hits you hard and there's not
          a damn thing you can do about it.
                    (an afterthought)
          In a way I admire them.
```

JEANNIE
What? I thought you of all people
would understand how I feel.

MITCH
They're putting it on the line. That
takes guts. They're not afraid.

She looks at him incredulously.

JEANNIE
What are you implying, Mitch? That I
am?

MITCH
. . . They're putting each other
first. Maybe that's why you're having
trouble with it.

JEANNIE
What do you want from me, to walk away
from my career, like Gloria, is that
where you're going with this?

MITCH
I love your passion Jeannie, but you
don't just write music because you
love it, you write because it doesn't
allow you room for anything else.

JEANNIE
You know what, Mitch? I'm giving you
the best I've got.

MITCH
No, you're not, I know you better than
that.

JEANNIE
Nobody's been asking you to stay.

She grabs her purse and walks to the door.

MITCH
Merry Christmas. Your gift's inside
your bag.

```
INT. HALLWAY — DAY

Jeannie leans against the door, reeling. She opens her
bag, and finds a small box. She opens it. It's an
engagement ring. She breaks down and cries.
```

What is the subtext in this scene? At the level beneath the dialogue, what is really being said?

- In the first speech, Mitch is really talking about himself and his underlying frustration with his relationship with Jeannie.
- Jeannie's threatened when he says he admires Gloria and Billy for putting it on the line. She's lost an ally, but more important, he's implying she's afraid, she doesn't have the guts.
- When Mitch tells her she's unable to put someone else first, she immediately uses her career as a defense. She's inferring he wants her to quit her career, which has never been the case.
- Mitch knows the depth of Jeannie's feelings, but she can't confess to them because she's afraid to commit, and so she leaves.

It has been said that writers either have an ear for dialogue or they don't. I believe this "ear" can be developed. Try to hear the dialogue as you write it. Visualize the actors delivering the lines.

Once the dialogue is written, read it out loud to yourself or to a partner. An amazing thing happens in the process; you will naturally edit excess or awkward wording. You will also become conscious of pacing and tempo. Turn on the television set and listen to shows rather than watch them. With your visual sense turned off, your ear becomes more in tune with the cadence and rhythm of the spoken word. We will study dialogue further in later chapters.

Camera Angles

Directors don't like to be told how to shoot their pictures. The misuse of camera angles is a dead tip-off that you are an amateur, even if the camera angles are correct. Too many of them make for a staccato read: they cut into the flow and momentum of the script. When can you legitimately use a camera angle? Only when it is absolutely needed to tell your story, but writers hardly use them at all anymore. Let's say, in a story you are scripting, a killer inadvertently drops a book of matches as he leaves a crime scene. Later these matches will incriminate him. The writer here could choose a "close on," but the easier way to go is to just write the action in the description: "The killer drops the book matches as he leaves." Camera angles are becoming unpopular these days. Scripts are becoming less and less cluttered. Most writers write in what is called the master scene format.

The *master scene format* is the "whole" picture. If your locale is INT. BEDROOM – DAY (also referred to as the scene heading or slug line) then we are looking at the entire bedroom; therefore, anything that takes place in that bedroom can be described in the action/narrative. It does not need a camera angle. Writers should not concern themselves with the camera; they should think about their writing!

We have now reviewed the tools of the scriptwriter: locales, narration/action, dialogue, and camera angles, the last having now been replaced by the master scene format. Together, these tools combine and create the scene—the major building block of the script.

THE SCENE

The *scene*, the building block of the script, is the unit of action that moves the story forward. Imagine a set of building blocks. As the blocks come together, they form the complete creation. In both teleplays and screenplays, scenes or blocks of action build together, one upon the other, to tell the complete story.

The technical definition of a scene is that it roots us in time and place. The scene heading establishes where the camera is set; it is either INT. (interior) or EXT. (exterior). It establishes the time as DAY or NIGHT. In most screenwriting software programs, this is called a *slug line*. Following the slug line is a brief description or action (the narrative or action) telling us what is happening inside the picture.

Look around you. Where are you? In your office? At home? Perhaps you're reading this book in the park, or you're on an airplane. Is it day or night? How would you set up the scene? The next step is to describe what's there, what is taking place in the locale. What is inside the picture you've created?

At this moment, I am in a small crowded terminal in Costa Rica waiting for a puddle jumper to take me to my brother's house in Tamarindo. How can I take you there? By constructing the scene.

```
INT. SMALL TERMINAL — SOMEWHERE IN COSTA RICA — DAY

The plane is late. It's hot and humid, and packed. Ticos
are yelling in Spanish, and tourists are getting socked
in colones for overweight luggage. Behind the check-in
counter is something that passes for a Christmas tree.
```

- At this point, if I chose to take you out on the tarmac, that would constitute another scene. Why? Because the camera would have to be physically moved.

```
EXT. TARMAC — DAY

A single-engine prop plane makes a scary approach,
crabbing in the crosswinds. It touches down, bouncing off
the tarmac.
```

- If you, the writer, now switched back to the terminal, that would be another scene. There should always be a purpose for the scene. It should never be excess. Perhaps one of your characters is a terrified middle-aged writer running out of the building in search of tequila.

The Purpose of a Scene

Every scene must move the storyline forward and advance the plot. If the scene does not reveal new and relevant story information, or reveal new aspects of your character or characters, it does not belong in the script, regardless of how well it may be written. It is fat and must go.

The scene must help the material as a whole. It must be an integral part of the story's continuity. Say it once and move on. If the scene repeats information we already know, then it belongs in the trash.

To help us better understand the power of the scene, let's return to the building blocks we used earlier. Imagine that your creation is now complete. The blocks have been placed in a particular order to give the whole story. Now, let's suppose you remove one of the blocks. If a hole isn't there (plot information missing or character insight gone), then the scene didn't belong there in the first place.

Types of Scenes

Scenes vary in length. They can run anywhere from a single shot to three and a half pages long. They technically could run much longer, but that is dangerous ground. Five- and six-page scenes are deadly. They kill the momentum and pacing of the script and are a tip-off that the writer has not yet grasped the medium of moving pictures.

There are exceptions to this rule. Aaron Sorkin's *West Wing*, for example, relied heavily on faced-paced bullet dialogue, and sitcoms use a different format, which will be covered in Chapter 6.

- *The establishing scene or shot* establishes where we are. It could be an exterior of Century City, LA, or downtown Chicago, or any place that roots the viewer to a place. Every week we see an establishing shot of Seattle Grace Hospital on *Grey's Anatomy*.
- *The dialogue scene* conveys information and reveals character, conflict, and feelings. An example would be the *Swing Sisters* scene on page 18.
- *The scene sequence* is a series of scenes tied together by a single idea. For example, look at Coulter finding

another abductee, on pages 14–15. The sequence consists of five quick scenes:

EXT. LOS PADRES NATIONAL FOREST – DAY
Establishes where we are.
INT. /EXT. A VINTAGE VOLVO – NIGHT
Coulter looks for an address.
EXT. THE MARTINEZ HOUSE
He finds it, but there is something strange about the house.
INT. MARTINEZ HOUSE – BEDROOM
We meet Jessie, who grabs an AK-47.
EXT. MARTINEZ HOUSE – NIGHT
Coulter spots the gun aimed at him.

Establishing sequences, dialogue sequences, and action sequences are explored fully in Chapter 7. Sequences essentially use the same components and serve the same purpose as the scene. Become aware of sequences as you watch television: they are a wonderful device for the scriptwriter. They are helpful in cutting between locales, maintaining continuity, and keeping the pictures moving. They also help you to identify larger blocks of story when stepping out your script.

The Crisis, Climax, and Resolution in the Scene Sequence

The scene and the scene sequence are essentially mini-units of the bigger whole. Within themselves they contain the same components as the script, just as the cell contains within it the same components as the universe.

All scenes (except for establishing shots) and sequences, have a crisis, a climax, and a resolution, but not all of it has to be shown on screen.

Let's suppose that we are constructing an action sequence in which the dramatic action is a car winding its way along an icy road. Suddenly, another car coming from the opposite direction spins out of control and careens over the center divider. The *crisis* is the build. At this point, the action could go either way, but an outcome is inevitable. The cars collide. The event is the *climax*. It is the high point of the dramatic action. The *resolution* is the result of the accident. What happens to the people inside the car? Do they live or die?

The luxury of writing for television or film is that the script-writer can cut into or out of the scene or sequence at any time. In fact, it is rare that a scene or sequence is shown in its entirety. Why? Because of the time factor. The scripter gives pieces or fragments that give the illusion of completeness.

If we're to use the above example, perhaps your choice would be to cut away from the scene at the crisis and leave the climax to the audience's imagination. Or perhaps you would choose to cut directly into the climax at the point of the sudden impact to jolt the audience. You could also come into the scene at the conclusion, or in the resolution, and only show the aftermath of the accident.

The scriptwriter is constantly making decisions. Each gives a different effect, a different feel. The best choices make the best scripts. Always ask yourself when constructing a scene or sequence what choice will have the most impact and best convey what you want to say.

Cutting between Scenes

Here is where contrast, mood, tone, and texture happen. A good writer can literally string an audience's emotions with one simple cut.

Paddy Chayefsky had a long and illustrious screenwriting career that began in television and eventually led to the motion picture Oscars. Among his works were *Marty*, *The Hospital*, and *Network*, which provided a satirical look at television networks and the people in power behind the ratings war. *Network* is considered a motion picture classic.

In the famous "mad as hell" sequence, Howard Beal, the television anchorman gone mad, yells to his viewers on prime-time television that they should go to their windows and scream, "I'm mad as hell and I'm not going to take it anymore!" It is magnificent writing by one of our greatest craftsmen. The sequence ends with incredible power: people screaming out in teaming, thunderous rain with the furor that, in Chayefsky's own words, sounds like a Nuremberg rally. He then cuts away at the climax of the scene, and in the next shot there is a plane descending on the runway. With that simple cut, we, the viewing audience, are being jolted from an emotional high. We are, essentially, through the airplane, being made to touch down again. His choice of cutting between these pictures is emotionally moving.

One of my favorite movies this year is the wonderfully written *Lars and the Real Girl*, about a lovable introvert whose emotional baggage has kept him from fully embracing life. Lars orders a life-size doll on the Internet that he names Bianca, and through his delusional relationship with "her" manages to heal himself. The writing is brilliantly crafted by Nancy Oliver. There is a scene in the movie when Lars's brother and sister-in-law go to their church committee and ask for their support. Lars's doctor, who believes his delusion with Bianca is a sign that he is working through some personal issues, asks could they please try and go along with it. Some members say they will support him; others think his behavior is deviant, like worshiping the golden calf. He certainly can't bring her to church, can he? They all turn to the reverend, who is torn. "The question is as always," says the reverend, "what would Jesus do?" The scene makes a quick cut to Lars singing in church. Next to him sits Bianca in her wheelchair, in her Sunday dress, with a hymnal in her lap.

Oliver ended the scene before its natural conclusion with the question, "What would Jesus do?" and then cut to the church for the visual answer, which provided all the humor.

Watch one-hour and two-hour television shows and movies. Become conscious of the power of the scene. See if you can identify not only the scene's structure but where it begins and ends and how the writer chooses to cut between scenes.

Study the best. Watch quality television and analyze it. Learn from the pros, from the writers who are selling. They will teach you a lot.

3.

RESTRICTIONS OF THE MEDIUM AND HOW YOU CAN MAKE THEM WORK FOR YOU

THE FIRST RULE OF TELEVISION writing is that you play by the rules until you are big enough to call the shots. For the television freelancer trying to break in, the rules have already been set.

Let's suppose you have decided to write for an already existing television series. In this series, the hero is a district attorney. You like the show but feel it's unrealistic that he wins his case each week. The show is slipping and, as far as you are concerned, it's time the writer came in with a fresh approach.

If the producers or story editors of the show would only read your script, you are certain they would be wowed. They will admire not only your writing but also your insight. Right? Wrong.

Any experimentation in television happens "in-house," meaning by the developers, the producers, and the staff of writers for that particular show. The television freelancer does not have the freedom to forge new trails but must rather take the established path. And herein lies the challenge.

To write a great script within these highly restrictive parameters is to give the show's creators and its "power people"—the producers and the network—what they want.

How can you do this? Since you can't change the beast, you must study it, tape it, watch it over and over, and buy scripts from the show (see Appendix A). Study the show for at least two seasons. This also proves the show's staying power. You'll discover that the show gives you everything you need to know: structure, characters, the age demographics of the audience, and even the storylines you can develop.

HBO takes pride in its innovative, bold, adult entertainment. They love pushing the envelope. Shows like *The Sopranos*, *Sex and the City*, *The Wire*, and *Six Feet Under* created the catch phrase "It's not TV, it's HBO." Showtime also sells "edge." If you choose to write a spec *Weeds* or *Dexter* script, then, obviously, you do the same and write it with "edge." FX is steadily moving up into those ranks with shows like *Nip/Tuck*, *The Riches*, and *Damages*, and now AMC with *Mad Men*.

The show will present its parameters; all you have to do is watch it. Write what the show sells. If profanity and nudity are used, then bring those elements into your script. If this kind of programming offends you, then don't watch it, and certainly don't attempt to write for it.

Network television is much more conservative because of network practices, but again, the show dictates your boundaries. I love the writing on *Brothers and Sisters*. It's a terrific family drama that deals with universal issues. Who among us is untouched by loss, addiction, infidelity, sexual or religious issues at some point in our lives?

Maybe you resonate with the zany, over-the-top *Pushing Daisies*, or the slapstick action comedy *Chuck*. Write for a show you know, you love, and you feel you can write well.

Writing a spec script and staying within a show's set parameters can be challenging, but it's also fun. When you think about it, a lot of the work has already been done for you.

I grew up watching *Kojak*. I never missed an episode, and this was before the days of VCRs. I knew every character in the Manhattan South precinct and just about every storyline that aired. I could even guess when the bald-headed lieutenant would pull out a lollipop! When the show was in its last year, I discovered that a woman I had become acquainted with who ran a kiosk on the Universal lot knew the story editor for the show.

I told my friend, an unemployed actress, Kathy Donnell, and together we decided to write a spec script for the show. Our original intent was to write in parts for ourselves, but they never materialized. The seed for the story took form when Kathy told me about a strange incident that happened at a party one night. Morticians had come to the door and informed the hostess that they were there to pick up her husband's body. The hostess was horrified by the prank, informed the men in black that her husband was fine, and sent them away. An idea struck me, what if, after the men left, the woman went into the study and discovered her husband with his throat slit? The result was a script entitled.

Death Is Driving You Home. In it, the killer had a bold M.O.: he would call the mortuary and request that they pick up a body before his victim was dead.

We were young and clueless. We had no idea how to write a spec script and nobody had told us how hard it was to get one sold. The only thing we knew was how hard it was to get an acting job. We wrote the spec using a *Hawaii Five-0* script for structure because it was the only cop show we could get our hands on.

After much hair pulling and many rewrites, Gene Kearney, the story editor, read our spec script. The show had been on the air for many years and the idea was clever and not derivative. He was impressed with how well we knew the show and all its characters. We even had a reference to Kojak's childhood red wagon that had been mentioned in a much earlier season. He commented on our dialogue, which I attribute to our acting background. He bought the script. I didn't know it then, but things like that aren't supposed to happen.

We thought, for the most part, the script would be shot as is. When we went for our first writers meeting we were in for a big shock. Kearney, the story editor, said there were so many plot holes in the story that the entire script needed to be restructured. We left with such copious notes that we drove to the nearest bar and stared at each other on overwhelm. After many rewrites, with Kearney's patient help, the holes were plugged, but the story became almost unrecognizable. We turned in a polished draft that the staff was happy with, and then after we left, the script was again rewritten and became even more unrecognizable. So began my career as a writer.

TIME LIMITATIONS

Television deals with highly restrictive time limitations. If the marathon runner can be equated with the novelist, the scriptwriter can be compared to the aerobicist. The teleplay writer has the leanest and meanest workout of all.

A teleplay is the bare necessities, the bones, the skeleton. It is the blueprint of visuals or fragments that give the illusion of the entire story. Television writing is so economical that every word in the script matters and must move the story forward.

There is no room in television for fat in the script. Everything nonfunctional must go! A novelist can say her book ran fifty pages longer than anticipated, but the story still works. This is not so for the teleplay writer. If you are off the mark, you give yourself away as an amateur.

Whether you are writing a half-hour sitcom, a one-camera comedy, an hour episode, or a two-hour movie for television, the writer must come in on the number of pages allotted to the show's time frame. I call this "coming in on the dime."

For example, an hour episode runs about one minute per page. Meaning, the writer must set up, develop, and resolve the storyline in about fifty-five pages. There are some exceptions to this rule, but they are rare. For example, the fast-paced *West Wing*, which relied heavily on dialogue, had teleplays that ran sixty-five to seventy pages.

Since episodic shows vary in page lengths according to their repartee and style, it is advisable to get your hands on an actual script for the show. You can download some scripts off the Internet for free and buy others at a reasonable rate (see Appendix A).

So how do you, the writer, come in "on the dime"? When I

first began writing, I was very intimidated by this requirement. I thought it was difficult enough to come up with a good story, let alone come in on the right number of pages.

I discovered, as time went on, that it is much easier than it appears. Once you study and understand format and structure, there are ways to start stepping out a story that will gauge for you how you are running (see Chapters 6, 7, and 11).

CHARACTERS ARE SET

Today's characters are richer and much more complex than they used to be. We, the audience, are fascinated by them. Unlike Jonathan and Jennifer Hart, they are richly flawed. How many of us liked Tony Soprano? His acts were evil, but he was a man in constant conflict, and we sensed in him a humanity that was in a constant struggle to be set free.

Who can be a bigger sleaze than Christian Troy in *Nip/Tuck*? Troy is an unconscionable opportunist, but he has a good heart. He cares deeply for his overly idealistic partner Sean McNamara, and he's devoted to their practice. Together, these two flawed characters make a complete whole.

Dr. House can be a mean S.O.B., but, hey, if I were dying, guess whom I'd call? Who's more emotionally tarnished than the Oklahoma cop in *Saving Grace*? And Nancy, the single mom in *Weeds*, who sells marijuana to make ends meet—she isn't exactly a pillar of society. Even the Walkers in *Brothers and Sisters* are pleasantly dysfunctional.

These characters come into our living rooms week after week and we, the audience, have a vested interest in them.

How many of us were waiting for and watched the last episode of *The Sopranos*? What was going to happen to Tony? Was he going to live or die? They were taking odds on his fate in Las Vegas.

For the show finale of *Six Feet Under*, there was a rumor floating around that everyone was going to die. A fitting end for a show about a family who runs a funeral home. But how were they going to pull that off? They did it, and it was nothing short of brilliant. If you haven't seen it, rent it—season 5, episode 12, "Everyone's Waiting." Young Claire loses her job offer in New York, but her dead brother Nate encourages her to go anyway and get out of the Fisher Funeral Home. Claire reluctantly goes. As she drives away in the last moments of the show, there are a series of flash forwards set over incredible music that show how each member of the family will live out the remainder of his or her life, and how they all will die. Claire lives to be a very old woman, surrounded by family, and we sense she has lived a contented, full life.

This was writing at its very best. It was an intimate, poignant end to Alan Ball's stellar series.

In writing the spec script, a writer needs to know all the characters on a show thoroughly and to write them into the script: not a small job, since there are so many ensemble shows on the air—*Boston Legal*, *Grey's Anatomy*, and *Lost* to name just a few. If the show uses the same characters week after week, then you, the writer, must utilize them also.

Sometimes characters will run on a show periodically; that is, they make an appearance now and then. That means in a spec script you can use them if you choose, but it is probably in your best interest not to. Let the in-house staff decide when to bring them back. Availability, cost, and many other factors enter in.

LOCALES ARE SET

Half-hour sitcoms shot live before studio audiences (three-camera shows) are very limited and restricted in their use of locales. These locales usually consist of three or four ongoing sets. Examples would be *Back to You*, *The New Adventures of Old Christine*, *The Big Bang Theory*, and *Two and a Half Men*.

On *Two and a Half Men*, the sets consist of Charlie Harper's living room, kitchen, a bedroom, and his mother's condo. If another set is needed for a particular story, it is called a *swing set*—that is, an existing set that is swung around and reset. Changing sets is expensive and takes time. Since these shows are taped live, in terms of both cost and time it is more efficient to keep the number of sets to a bare minimum.

Single-camera comedies like *The Office*, *Curb Your Enthusiasm*, and *30 Rock* are shot with one camera and can use locations. They are more expensive to make and have the look and feel of film. Again, the show will tell you where you can go.

Always ask yourself when developing an idea: can this story be told on the show's existing sets?

One-hour and two-hour shows are filmed using one camera and rely heavily on location shooting over and above their existing sets. The writer can now take the story anywhere in the city in which the show takes place.

If you are scripting an episode of *CSI: Crime Scene Investigation*, besides the existing sets, you have all of Las Vegas as your palette, just as in *CSI: New York* and *CSI: Miami*, the towns themselves become characters in the show.

Never relocate the show or transplant the characters out

of their established arena. It's a bad idea to take Deputy Chief Brenda Johnson and her team of detectives in *The Closer* out of LA and stick them in Minneapolis.

Successful shows can jaunt to another location perhaps once during the season. But watch the credits: I guarantee you that either the producer or the story editors wrote the show. Why? Because only they know how much money is in the till. To relocate the cast and crew is a highly expensive proposition. When it happens, it's the biggest show of the season, which guarantees it will not be written by a freelancer.

Don't say it doesn't matter because your spec script is just a sample of your writing; let the readers know you understand the way episodic TV works. Show that you are savvy, be content and keep your characters at home. Research the places in which they live. There are rich and unique locales in every city.

BUDGET LIMITATIONS

You don't need to make a detailed cost breakdown of the show, but use your common sense. If you are writing an action sequence and you have a choice of a car falling off a cliff or coming to a screeching halt and teetering on the edge, which will you choose? Practically speaking, the latter. Think in terms of the cost of production. In 2008, the average cost for a one-hour pilot was 2.5 million dollars! Again, the show will dictate your moves.

If it is an action show that relies heavily on elaborate stunts, then certainly you should incorporate these into your script. It would be a big mistake not to. Still, writers should always be conscious of budget. It would be a crime to write a good script and have them think you're clueless when it comes to budget.

After writing a *Hart to Hart,* I went in to pitch an episode the following season. In the series, Jonathan Hart was a pilot. The show sold glamour and a murder each week, so I developed a storyline around Jonathan and Jennifer at an air show. Certainly, it was a sexy enough backdrop.

The story editor almost choked. He said there was no way they could afford airplanes and stunt pilots. I got a job that season, but it certainly wasn't from that pitch!

Hart to Hart sold wealth, but always within budget. How? What about the Harts on a picnic? This would not be just any picnic. The fabulous-looking, very-much-in-love duo, who had perfect lives and no children, and who, unfortunately, stumbled onto a murder each week, would be sharing a bottle of outrageously expensive wine, eating caviar, with their Rolls Royce in the background. This scene conveys luxury without adding to the budget. Funny how they always managed to solve the crime while keeping the police at bay.

Characters are portrayed a little more realistically these days. Writing *The Riches* or *Dirty Sexy Money* certainly would be more fun!

Further Considerations Regarding Budget

Stay away from special effects if they do not exist within the format of the show. They are way too expensive. Avoid them at all costs.

Leave children out of the script. Unless they are regulars on the show, don't include them. I'm sorry if you're raising child actors, but I've learned over the years that stories involving children are a bad risk, and rightly so. Children, by law, are not allowed to work more than a limited number of hours. Also, they must have a guardian and school on the set, which can lead to shooting shutdowns and many other cost complications. In this industry, time is money. Once in a while a show will break down and, out of desperation for something fresh, develop a story around a child. Beware, however—it's a bad risk on a spec script. Again, show you're savvy by avoiding it.

Keep your exterior night locations to a minimum. Hollywood is locked in by the restraints of various unions and guilds. Night shooting means overtime, which can run into exorbitant costs. You do not have to exclude all exterior shots from your script. You should try to be economical, using only those shots that are crucial in telling your story. If the scene can just as effectively be shot by day, definitely write it for day.

My first attempt at a horror story was an episode of *Fantasy Island* entitled "Night of the Tormented Soul." The story was about a brother and sister returning to an old plantation house where they had been raised years before. Their fantasy was to learn the truth about a murder that had taken place while they were there—a murder so horrible that they had blocked the circumstances from their minds. They arrived at the haunted mansion at night in the teeming rain. Lightning was ripping and blasting away at the clinging vines growing over the entrance. A child's swing thrashed in the wind and falling trees blocked their way. It was quite an effective entrance. As it turned out, the scene was shot in broad daylight. There was no teeming rain, no lightning, and no falling trees. What was left in was the swing.

More recently, in a suspense thriller I scripted with writer Pamela Wallace for Showtime, entitled *Murder with Privilege*, we needed to keep all our night action sequences down to mostly interiors. Not much has changed on that front, except that the purse strings have gotten even tighter, and the cost of shooting has become exorbitant.

It is wise to be cost conscious, but at the same time, don't be so extreme that you diminish the impact of the spec material. Why would anybody want to read a horror story played out in broad daylight? Again, the writer must discriminate. If you are writing *Medium*, or *The Ghost Whisperer*, or any current drama that sells the supernatural, study how they squeak around the night shots. It will teach you a lot.

Leave out canines and critters of all kinds, unless they are running characters on the show. Here not only are you adding the cost of animal trainers and liabilities to the cast and crew, but there is the problem of defecation and more union people to clean it up. You'll also have Animal Rights and Doris Day to contend with.

In one of my *Hart to Hart* episodes, entitled "With These Harts I Thee Wed," Jennifer's auntie arrives on the doorstep with her pet Persian cat. Of course, the Hart's dog Freeway despises the furry creature throughout the show—until the end of Act IV, where the dog and the cat have become inseparable. When I turned in the script, the story editor deleted the entire bit, and one trainer and one Persian were back to looking for work. If you insist on putting a critter into your script, make it a fly. I used one once on a *Starsky and Hutch*, and the story editor kept it in. Flies don't come with animal trainers—they come with sound effects!

4.

THE HOOKS THAT SELL

WHEN YOU FINALLY GET THAT gold nugget, your first television assignment, you are on your way to becoming a member of the Writers Guild of America (see page 286). At this point you will have an agent representing you. If you don't, it's certainly time to find one! The agent's job is to know what shows are open for assignments. Unfortunately, today there are fewer and fewer; almost all shows are staff-written. But according to Guild rules, every show is supposed to have some freelance episodes open. They don't all have them, but some do.

The agent sets up a meeting with a show that is open, and you go in and pitch your ideas to the story editors and/or producers.

The fact that you got this far is a big step! You either have a legitimate writing credit (meaning you have already sold a script), or you have written spec material that has wowed an agent enough to take you on as a client, and he or she has submitted one of your scripts to a show that is impressed enough to want to meet with you. I hate the word *never*, but getting a pitch meeting without having an impressive spec script or having an agent doesn't happen, unless your godfather's named Vito Corleone, and the studio boss you're pitching to owns a racehorse named Khartoum.

The reason for pitching is twofold: First, you no longer have to write entire scripts before you learn what the studio bosses are interested in. (If pitching were not used, a writer could have ten *Shark* scripts stacked up in his garage.) Second, it shortcuts the staff's work as well: they will tell you what they're looking for. It saves time for everybody. You might have a good idea, but it's too close to something they already have in development, or it's derivative of an earlier episode. They may like certain elements of your story but make suggestions that could make the difference for a sale.

Pitching terrifies a lot of writers. They think they need the verbal skills of Barack Obama to walk away with an assignment. It's nice to be able to entertain, but if you don't have the story the studio heads want, then all you've done is manage to make their fifteen minutes with you a little more pleasurable.

I once asked my brother, who is very successful in sales, to speak at a marketing seminar I was giving for screenwriters. He asked the group what their goal was when they picked up the phone or walked into an office. Their unanimous response was to sell their scripts. "The first goal of marketing," he said, "is to get information. It doesn't matter if you're selling pencils, real estate, or screenplays, the person who gains the information gets the sale."

Besides walking out of a pitch room with an assignment,

the most crucial thing you can walk away with is information, because it's your open door. It allows you the opportunity to come back or to make that phone call. And when you do, this time it's with exactly what they want. In fact, it was usually on the second meeting that I landed most of my freelance jobs.

I didn't know it at the time, but the pitches I considered a total bust in the end turned out to be my biggest paydays. The contacts I made there and the people I stayed in touch with eventually moved on to other shows. They became my future employers.

My first pitch was for *The Streets of San Francisco*. I came in with what I thought was a good story, which I had rehearsed over and over. When the day finally came, I was a wreck, but I was prepared. I knew the story inside out.

The story editor nodded politely as I nervously talked, and when I was finished, he looked at me, and said, "You don't know our show." I turned bright red. He went on to say that *Streets* sold character, not crime. The show revolved around fascinating subsidiary characters, and I had come in with only a crime. In so many words, he was saying I had wasted his time.

I have learned valuable things through humiliation! It's easy to do in this business.

The next time I went in to pitch, it was for an episode of another cop show. This time I was really prepared. I not only had a good crime, I had wonderful subsidiary characters. But again, it wasn't enough. The story editor wanted the act breakdowns.

"What's the cliffhanger?" he asked. "And what do you see for the one and three act ends?"

I sat there stumbling around trying to cover. I was pitching way too much detail and not going for big climactic moments that build to the commercials breaks. Another big mistake. Again, I didn't get the job.

With each pitch meeting I would come in prepared with what I had learned at the prior pitch, but somehow it was never enough. There was always something missing.

I would come in with a good crime, good subsidiary characters, strong act ends, but the story editor said there were no twists and turns in the plot.

On one show they wanted more jeopardy, and on another a quicker setup. Another time, I was told my characters didn't have enough at stake. The next time, I needed more personal involvement for the stars. One producer wanted a better runner. *A runner?* This was getting ridiculous. When would it stop? I ran out in search of runners. *What the hell were they?* In the end, these pitching sessions did save me a lot of time, not to mention the trees that were saved from endless spec scripts.

After failing to get work, I slowly started learning what the producers and story editors were looking for. As diverse as these shows were, they all had similar needs. The story editors asked the same questions, had the same concerns, and wanted similar elements in their stories. I began to realize that television rested on certain *hooks*. Once I was able to identify these hooks, I started building my pitches around them, and that's when I started getting work. Why? Because I was giving them what they wanted.

New writers need not concern themselves with pitching. First, they must prove they can execute a script, and execute it well. Their focus should always be on the quality of their material. Pitching is the next step.

So why is learning these hooks so important? For many reasons; every time you turn on the TV, you can identify them, so your education will be ongoing. When you write your spec scripts, you'll know the devices TV rests on, and this will help you develop your story ideas. And when it's time for you to pitch, you will know what points to hit for a sale and not have to slog through trial and error as I did.

HOOK 'EM FAST

At the movies, we pay ten dollars plus to get in, and maybe more at the counter. If the popcorn is good and the reel isn't broken, we go into sensory overload with a 70-millimeter picture and THX sound that blows our eardrums out. Even if the movie is bad, we're highly unlikely to walk out.

TV is a whole different game. If we're dissatisfied, we've got hundreds of channels to choose from. It's called "let's go surfing." The Beach Boys sang about it.

The purpose of television is to grab viewers fast and keep their fingers off the remote, and when a commercial comes, to keep them hanging so they're pulled back from the refrigerator. Therefore, it is a medium that relies on hooks.

THE QUICK SETUP

The setup establishes what the story is about. It establishes everything we need to know to get the story moving. In episodic television, it is absolutely crucial that the setup happens quickly. Why? The sooner you get into the story, the sooner you hook your audience. Also, we are working with such terrific time limitations that unless the setup happens fast, there is insufficient time to develop the story.

The Half-Hour Setup

For the half-hour show, the setup for the A story, the most important story in the episode, is almost always complete by the first or second scene.

Two and a Half Men (a three-camera comedy): In the episode entitled "Old Flame with a New Wick," Charlie's old flame Jill comes for a visit. Charlie meets her in a bar and her name is now Bill. She has had a sex-change operation. The setup is complete. It happens in scene 2 of the script.

The Office (a one-camera comedy): In the episode entitled "E-mail Surveillance," Michael has called a computer technician into his office. We're not certain why, but it appears to be for some nefarious reason. When the technician leaves, Michael talks to the camera. He has decided to start reading his employees' e-mails. The setup is complete. It happens three minutes into the show.

Weeds (cable/Showtime): In the episode "Fashion of the Christ," Nancy's crazy brother-in-law arrives unannounced from Alaska. At the show's opening, there's the sound of pots and pans clanging in the middle of the night. The tired, pajama-clad Botwin family descends the stairs looking for the source of the noise. Nancy goes into the kitchen and discovers crazy Uncle Shane making an elaborate breakfast for everybody. She is not too happy to see him. On page one, the setup for the A story is complete.

One of the first comedies I had the pleasure of working on was *The Bob Newhart Show*. In the episode "A Day in the Life," Bob makes a bet that he can get out of town on a day's notice. In act 1, scene 1, the setup is complete; we establish what the story is about:

```
FADE IN:


INT. BOB AND EMILY'S APARTMENT


HOWARD IS ASLEEP ON THE SOFA WITH THE TELEVISION ON. BOB
EXITS FROM THE BEDROOM DRESSED FOR WORK. HE SHUTS OFF
THE TELEVISION AND SHAKES HOWARD.

                    BOB

          Howard, wake up!

                    HOWARD

          I think I just overshot Pittsburgh.

          What are you doing in my apartment?

                    BOB

          Howard, this is my apartment. You fell

          asleep in front of the television

          again.

                    HOWARD

          Oh, no! I missed it!
```

                              BOB

The end of the movie?

                            HOWARD

Channel 9's "Thought for the Day." Now

I won't have one.

                              BOB

Well, life's full of little

disappointments.

                            HOWARD

No, that was last Friday's "Thought

for the Day."

                              BOB

Ah. Well, I've got to eat some

breakfast and get to work.

                            HOWARD

Oh boy, breakfast! I'm so hungry!

                              BOB

Howard, keep it down. This is Emily's

first day of vacation, and I want her

to sleep. She's really tired.

EMILY ENTERS FROM THE BEDROOM DRESSED IN TENNIS WARM-UPS
AND SWINGING A RACQUET.

                            EMILY

(FULL OF ENTHUSIASM) Boy, I can't wait to

get to my tennis lesson. Gotta work on my

backhand, my forehand, and my footwork.

                    BOB

It's amazing what a little extra sleep
will do for you.

                   EMILY

Howard, did you fall asleep in front
of the television again?

                  HOWARD

'Fraid so.

                   EMILY

You didn't miss the "Thought for the
Day," did you?

                  HOWARD

Yeah, I did.

                   EMILY

Well . . . tomorrow is another day.

                  HOWARD

(GOES TO THE DOOR) That was two weeks
ago Wednesday. Well, I'm going to
freshen up. Gee, this is my lucky day.
I don't have to make my bed.

                    BOB

Why don't you make that your thought
for the day?

                  HOWARD

Thank you, Bob.

HE EXITS.

                    BOB

Want some breakfast?

                   EMILY

No, I'm just going to make myself a

health drink. Bananas, papayas,

pineapple, mangos . . .

THROUGHOUT THE FOLLOWING EMILY PREPARES A HEALTH DRINK
AND BOB STARTS PREPARING A BOWL OF CEREAL.

                    BOB

It sounds like you're going to eat

Carmen Miranda's hat. I thought you

were going to rest?

                   EMILY

I've decided to devote this week to

getting myself in shape, and this

drink is an important part of it.

Because, Bob, you are what you drink.

                    BOB

You had to tell me that just when I

fixed a bowl of Fruit Flakes.

THE PHONE RINGS.

                   EMILY

(WORKING THE BLENDER) Get that, will

you, Bob?

BOB

(ANSWERS IT: INTO PHONE) Hello . . .
(EXCITED)Peeper? Hey, Peep! Hi ya,
Peep! What d'ya say, Peep? (TO EMILY)
Emily, guess who this is?

EMILY

Prince Philip.

BOB

(INTO PHONE) When are you coming out,
Peeper? . . . You're not . . . We're
meeting you tonight . . . for a
week . . . in New Orleans.(TO EMILY)
He says we're meeting him tonight for
a week in New Orleans.

EMILY

Come on, Bob. It's another one of his
practical jokes.

BOB

(INTO PHONE) Peeper, when did you
start drinking this early in the
morning? . . . It's no joke? . . . But
that's crazy! I can't just pack up and
leave! Peep, I know it's a beautiful
city . . . Yes, great food . . . The
music, too . . . Al Hirt says he won't
play another note until I come? . . .

> BOB (CONT'D)

Peeper, my patients are booked. I'm

not a party pooper. I've been known to

be a wild man!

> EMILY

(LAUGHS) Yeah, you're a real

heck-raiser.

> BOB

Peep, I can be very spontaneous if you

give me a week or two to plan

it out . . . I'm an old lady, am I?

Well, I resent that, Peeper, and I'm

going to tell you so tonight in

person . . . Okay,

we'll be there. See ya.

HE HANGS UP AND LOOKS AT EMILY FOR A BEAT.

> BOB (CONT'D)

Emily, how would you like to beat your

feet on the Mississippi mud?

> EMILY

You know you hate to travel.

Usually wild horses can't pull you

away . . . The Peep makes one phone

call and you're out that door.

                                BOB

        Emily, you've got to be more spontaneous.

                               EMILY

        Really? Well, Mister Wild Man, what

        about all the appointments you've

        booked for next week?

                                BOB

        I'll reschedule them. I'll make all

        the arrangements. We'll be on a plane

        for New Orleans tonight.

                               EMILY

        (SMILES) I think I smell a bet.

                                BOB

        (SMUGLY) You name it.

                               EMILY

        Okay. Every year we have trouble

        finding somebody to play the Easter

        Bunny at the school egg hunt.

                                BOB

        What do I get if I win?

                               EMILY

        If you win, you get to spend a week in

        New Orleans with a beautiful,

        sensuous woman.

                    BOB

    Do I get to pick her? (OFF HER LOOK)

    Fair enough, Emily. Now . . . (RUBS

    HIS HANDS TOGETHER) what do I need to

    do first?

                    EMILY

    First we have to have you measured for

    your bunny outfit. Then you'll need to

    get airplane reservations on

    incredibly short notice.

HOWARD ENTERS.

                    HOWARD

    Hi, Bob. Hi, Emily. Breakfast ready?

                    BOB

    Howard, can you get plane

    reservations?

                    HOWARD

    I don't need reservations, I sit in

    the cockpit.

We now know what the story is about. We have established Bob's dramatic need, that is, he must try to leave town on one day's notice. Since the Newhart character lacks any semblance of spontaneity, this is a good hook. It will be hard on Bob. It will create conflict, and the bigger the conflict, the bigger the humor. (We will study the setup in greater detail in Chapter 6.)

"A Day in the Life" is listed on a DVD as one of Newhart's best. My partner and I received the sole writing credit, but sitcom writing is highly collaborative and much of the credit goes to the staff.

The Hour Setup

For the hour show, the setup takes longer. That is, it almost always happens in the first three to four scenes. This is especially true with procedurals.

Procedurals are shows that rely on outside events or clues to unravel their stories. At the show's end, the mystery, or problem, is solved and has closure. *House*, *Cold Case*, *Women's Murder Club*, and the *CSI* franchise are examples of procedurals.

House always opens with a *teaser* (the opening that happens before the credits), which establishes the A story.

In a recent episode, "Don't Ever Change," written by creator David Shore and Doris Egan, the teaser opens on a Hasidic wedding celebration. Guests joyously lift the bride up in a chair as they dance the hora around her. She loses focus, everything becomes slow motion. Blood seeps through her white bodice. She collapses.

Scene 1: The B story is established: House discovers Wilson is dating Amber, one of his medical team candidates, whom he calls a "cutthroat bitch."

Scene 2: House, who gives the relationship two months, is

shocked to learn from Wilson that they have been dating and have been hiding it from him. Wilson's only half joking when he tells House he was afraid he'd hunt him down in the halls if he knew.

Scene 3: House is given the stats on the thirty-eight-year-old bride. She's lost control of her bladder, there's blood in her urine, and she broke her leg from the fall. Her UTI is clear, her CT is negative, there's no sign of kidney cancer, no tumors, no stones, but her sodium level is very low. Endometriosis? It's a possibility, or no food; Hasidic Jews fast on their wedding day. The sodium, says House, could've been absorbed by a toxin already in her body. He wants her tested for carbonic acid. The team says that's crazy, that much toxin in her system means somebody would have tried to poison her. As he leaves, House says, "Check her innards for bad cells, and her home for bad karma."

The setup is complete. House and the patient have come together. Now House has to diagnose what's wrong with her. The A story and the B story have been established. The running time (not counting the commercial break) is four minutes. In the hour format, a teleplay runs approximately one minute per page: four minutes = four pages.

Serials like *Grey's Anatomy, Brothers and Sisters,* and *Desperate Housewives* have large ensemble casts and stories that develop over a period of time. The setup to these shows is more complex since they rely on parallel storylines. But even serials have quick setups. Tape one of the shows. Get a timer and a legal pad, and pencil in how many storylines are presented in the first four or five scenes. You will be astounded.

We will discuss setups in both half-hour and hour formats in Chapters 6 and 7 in greater detail.

THE STAR IS PIVOTAL

Television is the star's medium. If *24*'s antiterrorist, Jack Bauer, is saving us from a deadly threat, and he's hunted down in the process, then it must be Jack Bauer, using his own devices, who finds a way out. It can never be an outside force.

Week after week, fans of *24* waited for and watched Kiefer Sutherland come into their living rooms. Characters become very personal to audiences, and so too do the actors who play them. The tabloids prove that.

Who is the star of *24*—Jack Bauer or Kiefer Sutherland? In *Grey's Anatomy*, is it Dr. McDreamy or Patrick Dempsey? In *30 Rock*, is it Liz Lemon or Tina Fey? Did we tune in for James Gandolfini or for Tony Soprano?

Characters make the stars, and the stars make the characters. Like everything in Hollywood, it's collaborative; look at *Curb Your Enthusiasm*, where Larry David plays Larry David, and *Seinfeld* is a no-brainer.

Writers should always focus on the stars. It's what the show sells, and it's the writer's job to create the kind of material that shows off their skills.

In *The Bob Newhart Show*, it was Bob who had to get out of town on short notice—not Emily, not Howard down the hall, not Carol at the front desk, but Bob.

What Newhart is famous for are his monologues. The episode "A Day in the Life" allowed him numerous opportunities for monologues on the phone. A writer can't always hit on this; some stories you luck out on, and some stories just won't allow for it, but you can always try to write to an actor's strengths.

Know what the show sells. Is it two hotdog cops in a hotdog car (*Starsky and Hutch*), or a tour de force featuring one actor (*House* or *Shark*)? Does it sell edge and sex in a world of superficial beauty (*Nip/Tuck*), or three beautiful friends and the sacrifices they must make as women to stay on top (*Lipstick Jungle*)?

I'm sure you've seen reruns of *Three's Company*. This sitcom sold three twentysomething singles, Jack, Janet, and Chrissy, sharing an apartment in Venice Beach, California. The episode we wrote, "Coffee, Tea, or Jack," was Jack's story, but since the show sold three stars, Janet and Chrissy had to be pivotal to the plot.

The story is about an old flame coming back into Jack's life and turning it upside down. The girls create the mess Jack gets into, so now they must devise some plan to help him get out of it. It was Jack's story, but it became the trio's s problem. It would have played out the same way had it been Janet or Chrissy's story.

In *Two and a Half Men*, if the A story is Alan's, Charlie will always play a pivotal role.

The hour shows that once relied on car chases and stunts to keep the action going have now been replaced with ensemble casts, multiple storylines, quick cuts, and fast pacing. Shows like *Brothers and Sisters* and *Grey's Anatomy* are exceptionally well-crafted soaps. *Grey's* is not about people who work in a hospital, it's about the personal lives of a team of interns and the supervisors they work for. What's key are their personal conflicts, which run in every storyline.

Write to the stars and give actors their Emmy moments. And the harder you make it on their characters, the more the audiences will be rooting for them.

PERSONAL INVOLVEMENT FOR THE STAR

This is a wonderful device to hook your audience. It can't be done in every storyline, but it's great to have in a pitch or spec script.

What is personal involvement? The star/stars of your story have something personally at stake.

Let's say you are writing a detective show, and in the setup a body turns up in a motel room. You know the show, and it's been mentioned that the detective is divorced. His ex-wife has never been seen; she's backstory. Why not connect this murder personally to your hero? The cop gets a call and he goes to the scene. He walks past the police tape and goes inside. The murdered woman on the floor is his ex-wife!

Recently, a *Shark* episode opened with Shark and a public defender going at it in court. By the looks of things, it's not the first time.

In the next scene, they share a beer at a local bar and we discover they're longtime friends. As they leave, a car drives past and the public defender is shot. Shark learns later his friend didn't make it through surgery. Now, for Shark, it's personal.

When Dr. Bailey, on *Grey's Anatomy*, realizes it's her son being rushed into the ER, she has much more personally at stake than usual. The audience cares about Dr. Bailey; therefore, they care more about this story. It also gives the great Chandra Wilson an opportunity to show what she can do.

After writing a *Hart to Hart*, I went back the following season and was given a *springboard* (an idea that jump-starts a story) they wanted to develop. They wanted an episode to revolve around a wedding. At the act 1 break, the groom takes a bite of the wedding cake and dies. I hated it, but I certainly wasn't about to tell them that. I wanted the job.

I decided the wedding took place in the Harts' backyard, that it wasn't just any wedding but the wedding of Jennifer's favorite aunt. The groom who dies is now Jennifer's new uncle, and whoever killed him was on the Harts' invitation list.

I still hated it, but I got the assignment. Why? There was personal involvement for Jonathan and Jennifer. The crime scene was in the Harts' backyard; both the killer and the victim are connected to them. The place and circumstances directly rest on them.

TWIST AND TURNS IN THE PLOT

Producers and readers feed off twists and turns in a story. If you can give them something they didn't see coming, that is credible within the context of the show, they will always remember you. Too many scripts are predictable.

Twists can happen anywhere. It was a twist that got us the *Newhart* assignment.

After going through hell to get out of town at the last minute, Bob and Emily finally make it to the airport.

INT. AIRPORT WAITING AREA — GATE FIVE — DAY

                   BOB

      I must admit there were times today I

      didn't think I'd make it.

                 EMILY

      I'm proud of you, Bob. You know, you

      really are a wild man. (GIVES HIM A

      LITTLE HUG)

THEY START TO HAND THEIR TICKETS TO THE STEWARD. THE
PHONE AT THE DESK RINGS; THE STEWARD PICKS IT UP.

              STEWARD

      (INTO PHONE) Gate five . . . wait a

      moment. (INTO LOUDSPEAKER) Phone call

      for Dr. Robert Hartley.

               BOB

      I'm Dr. Hartley. (TAKES THE PHONE)

      Hello? Hey. Peeper, we're on our

      way. Jazz on Bourbon Street, Creole

      food . . . what's that, Peep? . . .

      It's one on us . . . because you're

      not going? . . . It's a gag . . .

      that's real funny, Peep. (TO EMILY) Do

      you believe that? He's not going.

                         BOB (CON'D)

          (INTO PHONE) Do you know what I've

          been through to get here? The

          rescheduling! The aggravation! The

          Swerdlows! . . . Well, listen,

          we're going anyway! You hear that,

          Peep? . . . and it's going to be a

          million laughs . . . (TO EMILY) Right,

          Emily?

                         EMILY

          That's telling him, Bob. Why don't you

          put our things on the plane. Let me

          give him a piece of my mind. SHE TAKES

          THE PHONE.

                         BOB

          Go easy with him, Emily.

BOB HANDS HIS TICKET TO THE STEWARD, PICKS UP THE
LUGGAGE, AND WALKS THROUGH THE GATE.

                         EMILY

          (WAITS UNTIL HE IS GONE; THEN INTO THE

          PHONE) Thanks, Peep . . . It worked

          like a charm . . . I owe you one.

SHE GRINS, HANGS UP, HANDS HER TICKET TO THE STEWARD. AS
SHE WALKS TO THE GATE, WE:

FADE OUT.

Good scripts rely on twists, turns, and the unexpected. In the *CSI* franchise and *Women's Murder Club* whodunit, twists supply the needed jeopardy and suspense that place the audience in the discovery process. Unexpected turns in the plot hook us into cable and prime-time serials like *Dexter*, *Grey's Anatomy*, *Lost*, and *Ugly Betty*. In comedy, twists and turns in the plot provide necessary conflict and irony to provide us with humor. When developing your script, ask yourself, What is the audience expecting here, and what can I do to surprise them?

POWERFUL ACT ENDS

The single most important hooks in television are the act breaks. This is where the show goes to commercial. Everything in TV builds to the *act ends*. They are one of the first things a writer *breaks down* (identifies) in the structuring process.

Feature films and novels build to one climax. In a half-hour sitcom, there are two or three climaxes per episode and, in the hour show, there are four, five, or six climaxes per episode, all depending on the network format (see Chapters 6, 7). The exception is cable (HBO/Showtime), with no commercials.

The act ends are really cliffhangers—a point where the danger builds, the stakes are raised, a twist occurs or a whopper question or discovery leaves the audience hanging:

Meredith learns that Dr. McDreamy has kissed Nurse Rose in the scrub room.

Foreman informs Dr. House that the treatment isn't making the patient better, it's killing him.

On the season finale of *Desperate Housewives*, Edie hangs herself.

A GOOD RUNNER

After countless pitch sessions, I learned never to come to a meeting without a good runner. What is a runner? A device that "runs," or pops up, throughout the story. Runners are very effective in half-hour comedies. You can always spot them; they can be a bit or even a joke that keeps playing out. In hour dramas, they can be either comedic or dramatic and often open a window into the character's personal life. A runner offsets the main story; it should not be confused with a subplot or a B or C story.

Imagine we are writing a TV series about a male and female detective. The female we'll call Lucy. Lucy is married with an eight-year-old daughter. In this week's episode Lucy and her partner are on the path of a treacherous serial killer (the A story). Lucy's partner, who is very uptight, is being called in for questioning by Internal Affairs on his handling of a murder suspect (the B story). Now, let's suppose that at the precinct Lucy checks her calendar and realizes she's forgotten about a parent-teacher conference for her daughter (the runner). Already she has had a run-in with the teacher, who she now suspects will think she's a negligent parent. Suddenly we are brought into Lucy's personal life. We are reminded that she is a wife and mother, a woman who juggles a career and a home. She's more than just a good cop and a good partner—she's human—and now we the audience can identify with her. Later in the show, we have the serial killer spotted while Lucy is en route to the rescheduled parent-teacher conference, and once again she's a no-show. Lucy must now deal with the terrific guilt. In the last beat of the runner, we decide, Lucy has the difficult task of finally meeting with the teacher.

I was once told by producer Joel Silver to always play out a runner three times. That was the magic number.

THE BUTTON

Just as act ends are important, so are scene ends. A *button* is a punch or an exclamation mark that helps the cut. In the *Newhart* script, Bob gets overly frazzled with having to make too many last-minute decisions. Emily arrives and asks where he'd like to go for lunch. "I don't care where," he says. "I just don't want to have to make any more decisions." At that moment, both elevator doors open at the same time. In this scene, the button is a visual joke.

A button can be a punch line of a joke, or it can hit hard on a point or problem to deliver a good act end.

In the pilot script for *The Closer*, at act 1 end, a very frustrated Deputy Chief Brenda Johnson lays into her team with a great monologue written by creator James Duff, who buttons it with a dialogue punch. "Because all we have right now, ladies and gentlemen, is a woman we can't identify, murdered by a man who doesn't exist."

Become conscious of buttons as you watch television.

Observe the different ways in which writers punctuate their scenes.

THE TEASER AND THE TAG

Teasers, or cold openings, and tags are written into the format of the show.

A *teaser*, as mentioned earlier, is the action that opens the show before the main titles and/or first commercial break. It literally does what it says—it teases the audience to stay tuned and not reach for the remote. *Pushing Daisies*, *Cold Case*, and *Ugly Betty* are examples of shows that open on teasers. The length of a teaser varies according to the show. It can run anywhere from one to ten minutes and often provides the hook for that week's story: we see the crime or find the body or are presented with character dilemmas or situations that will keep us watching.

The *tag* is the action that happens after the last commercial, ties up the loose ends, and wraps up the show. It can be light or dramatic, and in serials it can act as a teaser for the next week's show.

Some shows have no teasers or tags, some have both, some have one or the other.

Television comes in a multitude of formats these days and can get a bit complicated. Half-hour sitcoms, which once were almost always written in two acts, now come in two acts and three acts, and cable, with no commercials breaks, has no acts. The hour show that was once a simple four acts still exists, but now the five-act hour with a teaser is very common. And then there are the six-act dramas, mandated by ABC, like *Grey's*

Anatomy and *Brothers and Sisters*, which don't have a teaser or tag. But if you look closer, they really do: they are now act 1 and act 6 stretched out a little longer. And of course there is the hour cable show, which has no act breaks and reads like a small movie.

Have I made my point? I have seen blogs on the Internet with intricate discussions by spec writers on how to structure these shows. Yes, you must study them, and yes, you absolutely have to watch them. But just as important, cut to the chase, spend maybe twenty dollars, and buy a couple of episodes from the show. No instructor, no book, graphs, or charts, no chats on blogs can shortcut your time, be as accurate, or give you as much as the actual scripts themselves. These scripts are very easy to get your hands on. I use Script City; they're fast, and they can get me almost anything I want and send it the day I ask for it in a PDF file. There are other places as well (see Appendix A).

Study from the writers on the show!

They do it, you do it. They don't do it, you don't do it. It's that simple!

5.

THOUGHTS TO CONSIDER
BEFORE WRITING YOUR SPEC

WRITERS ARE TOLD NOT TO write a spec script for a series they want to pitch. There's good reason for this. The producers of that show will be the most critical of your work. Agents will send your specs to other shows where you'll be better received.

There's another way to look at it. Write a spec for the show you know you can write best. At this point you don't know what shows will be open for pitches. Your goal now is to get your writing noticed. Add this spec to your portfolio, or while it's being passed around, watch everything on TV that's in your genre (half-hour or hour), so when the opportunity presents itself, you can pitch to a number of shows.

I was very fortunate to make a good living at freelance writing and work for a wide variety of shows.

Today writers can't make a living as freelancers. Everything is staff-written and that's where you want to be. It's certainly where your agent wants you, because that's where all the money is, and your agent makes 10 percent of it.

If a show buys your pitch, and they are happy with the script you deliver, they almost always invite you back. If you deliver drafts equally good on a second or third assignment, your chances are very good for getting on staff.

The producers of *Starsky and Hutch* were so happy with our script that the next season they offered us a three-script commitment, but by then, we were too busy with other assignments. We had suddenly unplugged a dam. All the calls we had made in the two previous years began paying off.

To this day, I believe those two years of unemployment were possibly the most productive time of our partnership. Why? Because it's when we planted all the seeds, we never stopped, we never let up, and it was this perseverance, more than talent, that led to the jackpot.

Looking back, I've learned a very valuable lesson that I always share with my students. It's foolish to judge your successes by what is materializing at the moment. If you've laid the groundwork it eventually pays off.

Kathy and I had moved on to writing movies of the week (M.O.W.'s) and backdoor pilots (movies that set up TV shows). Had we looked into a crystal ball, we would have seen that this wasn't a good career move. Getting on staff and working our way up the series ladder would have been far smarter, but at the time it was one step closer to our dream, being feature film writers.

Today, TV is a tougher nut to crack. Many agents have out-of-work TV writers whom they are looking to place on staff, so reading spec TV episodes is not high on their to-do lists. This is why your writing must be more than just good; it must stand out.

I have critiqued many TV specs, and too often I come across good writing with mediocre ideas.

In television, the idea is king. The story you choose to develop for a particular show is absolutely essential to being noticed. Don't think because your spec is a sample and not intended for a sale that originality is not crucial.

Television agent Mitchel Stein says that while different producers are always on the lookout for different types of writers, all producers want writers with fresh ideas.

Television is fast. Producers need product. They have an entire season of episodes to fill. Week after week these shows have to be knocked out. They need writers who they know will come up with something good in the writing room.

There are thousands of writers out there who are already on the inside. These writers have agents who are sending out their material and setting them up with countless meetings. Your spec needs to be fresh, unique, and original. And it needs to have a voice and that takes work.

Showrunner Kevin Falls says, "Read a lot of writers—novelists, journalists, sure—but mostly screenwriters. Great TV and screenwriters have a specific voice to those execs who read scripts in town and make decisions that impact a writer's future. For a new writer, it's the prose that captures the attention of a potential agent or showrunner staffing a show. I look for a confident voice, an ear for dialogue, and deft storytelling."

Find what sets you apart from other writers. It's hard to define, but easy to spot. By the second or third page readers say to themselves, "There's something special about this writer." It's not enough to watch mediocre television and say, "I can do that." You need to look at the best shows and say, "I can do that or even better." Use the best of television for your measuring stick.

A number of years ago I had the privilege of judging a TV comedy writer's contest in Palm Springs, California. A well-known producer of a sitcom told the audience of writers, "Don't give me what I already know; give me some insight into my characters I haven't discovered yet. Those are the kinds of writers I am looking for!"

We already know that Dexter is a sociopath, and House can be a son of a bitch, and that the matriarch, Dora Walker, in *Brothers and Sisters* is the glue that holds the Walker family together. But can you find new insight into what makes these characters tick? These are the scripts that make producers take notice.

Don't be so eager to write that you settle for anything less than the best you can give. Don't settle for an idea until the hairs on your arm stand up. And don't turn in a script before it's ready.

My partner and I were exceptionally lucky to sell our first spec script, but if you don't pay on one end, you end up paying on the other. Two years went by and we had not gotten another job. A day didn't go by when we didn't make a call or try to get in to pitch somewhere. Everything in the beginning was closed to us. My former husband said it was time I started looking for another line of work; we had just bought our first home and I wasn't in any way helping to support it. When the pitch opening came on *Starsky and Hutch*, I needed that job. I racked my brains for a great idea, I prayed, I read everything I could get my hands on. One day I came across a quote by Joe Naar, the producer of the show. At the time *Starsky and Hutch* was being highly criticized for being the most violent show on TV. Naar responded to all the criticism by saying his responsibility was for authenticity. For undercover cops on the LA streets there was and always will be brutality. How much violence was too much violence, and where exactly does one draw the line between realism and responsibility?

Something struck me. If I could develop a story that defended Mr. Naar's point of view, we'd certainly have a shot at getting the job.

The problem was, how could we make this notion work? The show sold two hotdog cops in a hotdog car. That meant we had to put somebody else in the car to witness the action. A man would be an intrusion. A woman implied fun, because the guys would be competing for her attention. We decided to make the woman a reporter. Her intentions are different from what she says they are. At act 2 end, the first installment of her two-part article is scathing. She exposes the cops' roughhouse tactics as bravado and belligerence hiding behind the badge.

Now the problem was, How do we change her point of view? What happens that changes her mind? At act 4 end the A story and the B story dovetail (come together) with a twist. Starsky and Hutch rush to the abandoned building where they track down the suspect. They tell the reporter to stay in the car. She doesn't listen and gets in the way of the stakeout. The suspect grabs her and holds a gun to her head. She screams, "Shoot him!" Instead, the cops very slowly lay down their weapons and artfully talk the suspect into handing over his revolver, which saves her life.

We walked out of the pitch room with a job. Where do ideas come from? They come from everywhere. All you need to do is observe your world. Read every publication you can get your hands on: the newspaper, tabloids, and magazine articles. Watch *Oprah* and *The View*. Be on top of what is going on. What is timely? What is relevant right now? Observe your world as a writer does. If a problem is happening to you, could this problem or situation be happening to your characters in your show?

Find a springboard that resonates with you and play with it. Make it a game. Bounce the seed around while shaving or waiting in a line somewhere. Talk it out with friends.

Does your notion lend itself to the hooks? Ask yourself, Whose story is this? Does it play to the stars? Who drives the show? What about the setup—can it happen fast? Is there personal involvement? Does your idea lend itself to twists and turns in the plot? Is the idea contrived? Does it create big enough conflicts? Is it credible? Does it fit the characters on the show? Is it too similar to something that has aired on the show? If it is, it's a bad bet. Move on. Nothing at this point is written in cement. That's the fun of the creative process; like clay, you can keep molding one idea and retooling it.

Witness your world as a writer. Be conscious of everything around you. Life literally hands you things on a platter. It's fodder for something wonderful. Recognize these moments when they come.

I remember sitting at my computer one day stumped on how to end a scene. It needed a good button. In it, my protagonist, Alex, a former CEO gone bankrupt, is screaming on the phone trying to realign his credit. He can't take it anymore and slams down the receiver.

At that moment there was a knock at my front door. I answered to find two very solemn-looking men, dressed in black, holding Bibles. They had come, they said, to discuss their feelings on the end of the world. I gave them a donation and sent them on their way. Something clicked for me. I knew exactly what I needed.

Alex slams down the phone. He tries to get a grip, takes a breath, and says to himself, "Bankruptcy is not the end of the world." There's a knock at the door. He opens it to reveal two pale-faced men, dressed in black, holding Bibles. They've come to discuss the end of the world.

6.

WRITING THE HALF-HOUR SITCOM

OUR FIRST SITCOM ASSIGNMENT WAS for producers Tom Patchett and Jay Tarses for the MTM show *We've Got Each Other*. Patchett and Tarses were a very successful comedy-writing team who produced Bob Newhart and later went on to become creator/producer/showrunners for their own sitcoms, Jay Tarses for *The Days and Nights of Molly Dodd* and Tom Patchett for *Alf*. They gave us the best advice I've ever been given about writing comedy: writers should never try to be funny.

These men wrote very funny. Their scripts had kept us laughing for years. And yet, what were they saying? When writers work at being funny, they write for the joke or the punch line, and this is deadly. Instead, they told us, writers should create a story with so much conflict and with so many obstacles that the situation is funny. This input was invaluable, a weight was lifted off our backs, and we were freed from the terrible burden of trying to make people laugh.

Too often I've read comedy specs where the writers try too hard to be funny. You can feel their sweat as they force themselves to come up with three to five jokes per page.

Gag writing is a very special talent. Writers who come up from the ranks of stand-up, or people who write for late-night talk show hosts have it, and when it's spotted, those writers are gobbled up fast. It's a wonderful ability to have, but it's not a prerequisite for writing comedy, nor is being an unusually funny person.

Humor in the situation comedy comes from character and conflict. This is what Patchett and Tarses were saying.

Let's return to the Newhart pitch. Newhart had three very successful shows on the air; in all of them he played the same character. Newhart didn't have a spontaneous bone in his body. Putting him in a situation where he had to leave town on a day's notice would be an impossible situation for him. The producers responded to it. The situation provided the laughs.

COMEDY AND COLLABORATION

Comedy writing is a highly collaborative effort, much more than writing for the hour show. Even as freelancers we spent hours in the writing room stepping out the story with very talented story editors. We took copious notes and had a tape recorder rolling. When we went home, we'd go through it all and put it together. For every step in the development process we had input. We wrote a first draft, a second draft, and then turned in a polished script that they were very happy with. As freelancers, our job was now over. Theirs wasn't. Now they would begin rehearsing the show and "tooling it," nuancing it and making improvements with staff writers on the set, making adjustments as the actors needed. On day five, the show was shot live in front of an audience. Always sitting in the audience were the few freelancers lucky enough to get the job (the show was mostly staff-written), anxious to see how much of their material remained. Our jokes were punched up and the script sang. The writers took it up notches, and then a big surprise came: they'd added a new element to the story, so the last two scenes of act 1 we didn't even recognize. Most retooling has nothing to do with the writing itself. It is beyond the writer's control.

We learned this while working on *The Tony Randall Show*. In it Randall played a widowed somewhat exemplary judge living in Boston with his son and a British housekeeper. The episode we wrote, entitled "Case: Franklin vs. Casanova," was about Judge Walter Frankin discovering that his stoic secretary was dating the courthouse Casanova, Charlie Finmore. The judge, certain of his vast knowledge of human nature—and women—feels it's his duty to warn his secretary of the danger-ous course on which she has embarked.

The role of Finmore in our script was originally quite small. After we turned in the final draft, the actor they wanted to cast would only commit to the role if it was bigger. This changed the structure significantly. By the time we watched the taping, we were counting our lines on our fingers!

WRITING FUNNY: CAN IT BE TAUGHT?

Some professionals say yes. Others believe it is an inner sense that cannot be passed on. Comedy has a tempo and rhythm just like a piece of music. I believe that many writers can develop a better comedic ear through practice, and that only some are born with perfect pitch.

Comedy and drama are essentially the flip sides of the same coin. They both rely on conflict to move the action forward. The only difference is the point of view. The comedy writer sees the situation from the comedic P.O.V. and the drama writer from the serious. Yet the situations they are writing about can be identical.

For example, in an episode Larry David wrote for *Curb Your Enthusiasm* entitled "Special Section," Larry returns home to discover his mother has died and was buried two days earlier. While trying to move her to a better section of the cemetery he discovers he can use her loss to get out of a number of unappealing invitations, and the result is hysterical.

Comedy bites and makes fun of human imperfection. Situation comedy thrives on it. We laugh at Seinfeld, Ray Romano, and Larry David when they are forced to come face to face with their own shortcomings. Comedy magnifies their character flaws, and we, the audience, identify with them.

STRUCTURE: THE MOST ESSENTIAL ELEMENT

There are two types of sitcoms. The traditional multicamera (usually shot in front of a live audience) and the single-camera, which is shot very similarly to the one-hour shows.

The multicamera show is almost always in two acts, each act consisting of approximately four to six scenes. The format for these shows is different from the screenplay and one-hour teleplay format, where the rule is one page equals one minute. Half-hour scripts are typed double-spaced; each page equals about thirty seconds of tape or film. The scripts run about forty to forty-seven pages.

Single-camera shows use the one-hour format. Most of these scripts are written in three acts, but not all of them, the exception being cable shows, which have no commercials. Single-camera shows have both standing sets and locations. The scripts run about twenty-eight to thirty-five pages, and the scenes vary according to the act structure.

I'm only giving approximations here, because each sitcom has its own specific format. This is why it is imperative that you read scripts from the sitcom you choose to spec out.

Regardless of how the formats vary, the running time for these shows is the same—about twenty-two minutes.

In the half-hour sitcom, the setup must be complete by the first or second scene. In the *Newhart* you read, the setup was established in scene 1. From this point on, all the humor in the script comes from the obstacles placed in Bob's way.

Character + Dramatic Need + Obstacles = Conflict = Laughter

Let's pick up where Bob arrives at work.

SCENE 2

INT. RECEPTION AREA

CAROL IS AT HER DESK. THE ELEVATOR PINGS AND BOB GETS OFF.

                    BOB

          Carol, I'm on my way to New Orleans.

                    CAROL

          You took the wrong elevator.

                    BOB

          Emily and I are going to spend a

          week's vacation down there.

                    CAROL

          A week's vacation? Now see here. We're

          trying to run a business, my friend,

          not a Holiday Inn. We can't have

          people coming and going at the drop of

          a hat, now can we? What do you have to

          say for yourself, Hartley?

                    BOB

          You're fired.

                    CAROL

          You need a vacation.

                    BOB

          Welcome back. (THEN) Now look, I've

          got this all worked out.

BOB (CONT'D)

(PULLS A PIECE OF PAPER OUT OF HIS

POCKET) I'm going to transfer some of

my patients to Dr. Walburn. The others

we have to double up the week after

next. Thusly . . . (READING) Move Mr.

March to two o'clock . . .

CAROL

He works afternoons.

BOB

Scratch that. (TEARS OFF THE TOP STRIP

OF PAPER) . . . Put Mr. Voltz at

three . . .

CAROL

Bob, you know, Mr. Voltz is terrified

of the number three.

BOB

Oh, that's right . . . (TEARS OFF

ANOTHER STRIP OF PAPER) Shift Mrs.

Slater to Thursday . . .

CAROL

She lifts weights on Thursday.

BOB

Of course. (TEARS OFF MORE

PAPER) . . . Put Mr. Harris on

Friday?

                        CAROL

        Uh, Bob . . . Mr. Harris on Friday?

                        BOB

        (GETTING HER POINT) Oh, right. (RIPS

        ANOTHER STRIP OFF) And put Peterson in

        the morning . . .

                        CAROL

        That's okay.

                        BOB

        Fine. (HANDS HER ONE TINY BIT OF

        PAPER) You fill in the gaps.

                        CAROL

        Right, Bob. (THEN) Mr. Carlin is in

        your office.

                        BOB

        Again?

                        CAROL

        He's been waiting there an hour.

                        BOB

        Sometimes I don't know whether to

        charge him fees or rent. (OPENS HIS

        OFFICE DOOR) Carol, get me Dr. Walburn

        on the phone.

And as he exits into his office, we reset to scene 3.
Here we present Mr. Carlin, who is the B story. At the time

I was writing this script, I was reading a book on positive thinking, which recommended its readers spend a day listing all their negative thoughts. This little exercise worked wonderfully for this scene.

Mr. Carlin presents Bob with yet more obstacles.

                              SCENE 3

INT. BOB'S OFFICE

BOB ENTERS. CARLIN IS ON THE COUCH.

                              CARLIN

          What you want with Walburn?

                               BOB

          Hello, Mr. Carlin. I'm going to be

          leaving for a week, and I'm going to

          refer some of my patients to him.

                              CARLIN

          Not this patient—Walburn's a turkey.

                               BOB

          Walburn is a very reputable doctor.

                              CARLIN

          He hates me.

                               BOB

          Dr. Walburn doesn't hate you. You just

          got off on the wrong foot.

                    CARLIN

It wasn't my fault about the hamster.

How was I to know it was his pet?

                    BOB

Putting a little bit of cheese on a

mousetrap is not feeding.

                    CARLIN

Well, he went for it.

THERE'S A BUZZ ON THE INTERCOM.

                    BOB

Yes?

                    CAROL

Excuse me, Bob. Dr. Walburn's on the

phone.

                    BOB

Thanks, Carol. (THEN) One moment, Mr.

Carlin.

HE PICKS UP THE PHONE.

                    BOB (CONT'D)

Hello, Frank . . . How are you? . . .

Good. I'm calling because I'm going

away. Can you cover for me next week?

The regulars and the group . . . Yeah,

Mr. Carlin will be there too . . . You'd

rather be staked to an anthill? . . .

Listen, Frank, if you'll remember,

I took care of your patients last

fall and, as I recall, I had a lot of

trouble with that hockey player . . .

I don't care if she is a nice lady off

the ice. You still think Carlin's worse?

You'll gladly take the rest of them?

Well, good, I really appreciate it,

Frank. . . . Good-bye. (HE HANGS UP.)

                    CARLIN

He's still sore at me about the rat.

                     BOB

I have a suggestion, Mr. Carlin.

                    CARLIN

Nothing doing, Hartley. I can't go a

whole week without a session.

                     BOB

Well, I could call you up and we could

have sessions over the phone.

                    CARLIN

Not a chance. How would I know if you

were making faces at me?

                     BOB

Well, if that's the way you

feel . . . I guess I'll have to call

off the trip.

                         CARLIN

    I'll tell you what. If you're gone for

    a week, then you owe me five sessions,

    right?

                         BOB

    That's right.

                         CARLIN

    Then you can give me all of them today.

                         BOB

    Five sessions or an Easter Bunny.

                         CARLIN

    Take it or leave it.

                         BOB

    Then I guess we'd better get started.

    Where did we leave off last time?

                         CARLIN

    You told me to get a notebook and keep

    a list of all my negative thoughts.

CARLIN OPENS UP HIS NOTEBOOK.

                         CARLIN (CONT'D)

    Where do you want me to start?

                         BOB

    Let's take it from the top.

                         CARLIN

    Number one, a dollar ninety-five for

    the stupid notebook . . .

On Bob's reaction, we dissolve to scene 4.

A scene establishes place and time. Here we are at the same locale, Bob's office, but it is an hour later. The transitional camera technique most commonly used to do time change is called a *dissolve*. Notice how the dialogue serves to connect the scenes and helps the time lapse.

SCENE 4

INT. BOB'S OFFICE — 1 HOUR LATER

CARLIN IS STILL READING FROM THE NOTEBOOK.

                    CARLIN

        Six hundred eighty-seven, my pajamas

        itch . . . Six eighty-eight, what if I

        fall asleep and don't wake up . . .

                    BOB

        Has this list taught you anything

        about yourself?

                    CARLIN

        Yes, I'm not a happy man . . . but I'm

        very observant.

                    BOB

        Don't you feel you're a little too

        negative about everything?

                    CARLIN

        No.

```
                        BOB

        Why don't we pick it up next time,

        okay?

                      CARLIN

        So, what I should remember is not to

        take all these things so seriously.

                        BOB

        Exactly. Like my going away.


    CARLIN OPENS HIS NOTEPAD, BEGINS WRITING.

                      CARLIN

        Number six hundred eighty-nine,

        Hartley abandons patient.


    THEY EXIT TO:
```

Here a new element is introduced into the story: the Swerd-low family.

The Swerdlows were written in at the last minute, long after my partner and I had turned in our script. They were not our creation but that of the staff writers who were working on the show at the time. The producers originally wanted a scuba diver to step off the elevator in full gear for a session with Bob. He was a twin and having an identity crisis with his brother. When we arrived for the taping of the show, we were told that they had found something that worked better in rehearsals.

                              SCENE 5

INT. OUTER OFFICE

BOB AND CARLIN COME OUT.

                         CARLIN

          Who is the next group?

                          BOB

          It's a family. The Swerdlows.

                         CARLIN

          You're treating a whole family?

                          BOB

          Well, when they came to see me six

          months ago, they had tremendous

          hostilities toward each other. They

          were arguing and fighting.

                         CARLIN

          Makes me feel kind of homesick.

                          BOB

          But lately they've really started making

          an effort to get close to each other.

THE ELEVATOR DOORS OPEN AND THE SWERDLOWS ARE STANDING
THERE, MAN AND WIFE AND TWO TEENAGE KIDS. THEY'RE POSED
JUST LIKE AN OLD-FASHIONED FAMILY PORTRAIT, STANDING
VERY CLOSE TO EACH OTHER.

                    SWERDLOWS

          (IN UNISON) Good morning, Dr. Hartley.

                      BOB

          Good morning.

                    FATHER

          (TO HIS WIFE) After you, honey.

                    MOTHER

          No, no, the children must go first.

                      TOM

          No, Mother, after you.

                     BECKY

          Yes, we insist that our beloved

          parents . . .

THE ELEVATOR DOOR CLOSES.

                     CARLIN

          It's a good thing they were not on the

          Titanic.

THE DOORS OPEN AGAIN.

                    MOTHER

          Silly us.

                    FATHER

          Okay, everybody move out at the same

          time.

THEY ALL PUT THEIR ARMS AROUND EACH OTHER AND STEP OFF
THE ELEVATOR IN UNISON.

                        BECKY

Wasn't that a pleasant elevator ride?

                        TOM

I particularly enjoyed the sixth

floor.

                        MOTHER

The important thing is that we all

rode together.

                        BOB

Mr. And Mrs. Swerdlow, Tom, Becky, I'd

like you to meet Mr. Carlin.

CARLIN SMILES AT THE SWERDLOWS' ADLIB HELLOS.

                        BOB (CONT'D)

Mr. Carlin, I'll be done in an hour.

(TO THE FAMILY) Shall we go into the

office?

                        BECKY

Oh boy, another session!

                        TOM

We love Dr. Hartley's office.

                        BECKY

We love Dr. Hartley.

THE SWERDLOWS GO INTO BOB'S OFFICE. BOB FOLLOWS THEM IN.

We are now building to our act 1 end. It appears at this point that Bob has solved his problem with Carlin. But as we'll soon discover, this problem will lead to a greater complication, on which we end act 1.

SCENE 6

INT. BOB'S OFFICE

THE SWERDLOWS ALL SIT ON THE COUCH. CARLIN COMES IN BEHIND BOB AND, UNSEEN BY BOB, SITS ON THE COUCH WITH THE FAMILY. BOB CLOSES THE DOOR, THEN TURNS AROUND AND SEES CARLIN.

                    BOB

     Mr. Carlin, what do you think you are

     doing?

                    CARLIN

     This will be one of my sessions. I

     wouldn't miss this for the world.

                    BOB

     Absolutely not. You can't stay. This

     is not your session.

                    FATHER

     Please, Dr. Hartley. If he'd like to

     stay, I'd like him to stay. We want

     nothing here but good feelings.

                    MOTHER

Since we've been coming to Dr. Hartley,

we've been trying to like everyone.

                    BOB

Well, this will be your first big

test.

                    TOM

You are a beautiful person, Mom.

                    BECKY

Don't forget Dad, Tom.

                    TOM

He is beautiful too.

                    CARLIN

Am I dreaming this?

                    BOB

If you're going to stay, Mr. Carlin,

please be quiet. (TO THE FAMILY) Well,

I want to tell you how pleased I am

that you're no longer fighting, and

that you're working so hard to get

along . . .

                    MOTHER

We're doing our best.

                    BECKY

We couldn't do it without you, Dad.

He's a gem.

                    FATHER

Well, I'd be lost without all of you.

You're the best family a man's ever

been blessed with.

                    MOTHER

Amen.

                    CARLIN

Hartley, somebody's trying to put you

on.

                    BOB

Mr. And Mrs. Swerdlow, Tom and Becky,

it's good for a family to cooperate,

but it's also important not to hide

our feelings. Imitating a happy family

is not the same as being one.

                    FATHER

But we love each other, Dr. Hartley.

You've shown us that love is better

than hostility.

                    MOTHER

God bless you, Dr. Hartley.

                    TOM

God bless us and everyone.

                    CARLIN

(TO BOB) You're treating the

Stepfords.

                    BOB

Mr. Carlin, if you don't be quiet,
you're going to have to leave. (THEN
TO THE SWERDLOWS) Some patients
overreact to therapy. They go too far
the other way.

                    TOM

Could I say something, Dr. Hartley?

                    BOB

Of course, Tom.

                    TOM

I made a decision today. I'm going to
sell my motorcycle, give up the guitar,
and go into business with you, Dad.

                    FATHER

Oh, son! (HUGS TOM HAPPILY)

                    BOB

Mr. Swerdlow . . . you are a mailman.

                    FATHER

Yes, Dr. Hartley ...you're right. But
Tom can take one side of the street
and I'll take the other.

                    CARLIN

(TO BOB) These people could win the
Pillsbury Bore-off. (TO THE SWERDLOWS)
You can't fool me. No family's this
happy.

                    BECKY

That's not true. We are as happy as we

can be.

                    CARLIN

I think you're out of your tree.

                    BOB

All right, Mr. Carlin, that's it. You

have to leave.

                    CARLIN

Okay, I'll go.(RISES AND GOES TO THE

DOOR) But tell me, Dr.

Hartley . . . have you broken your

news to the Waltons here?

                    MOTHER

What news, Dr. Hartley?

                    FATHER

I'm sure if it's Dr. Hartley's news,

it'll be delightful.

                    BECKY

He's finally going to come to dinner!

THEY ALL CHEER.

                    TOM

What'll we have?

                    MOTHER

I'll fix him my special fried chicken.

                              BECKY

          And apple pie!

                              TOM

          I'll say grace.

                              FATHER

          And plenty of good, fresh milk.

                              CARLIN

          Hartley is leaving town next week, and

          leaving you in the lurch.

A DEADLY SILENCE FALLS OVER THE ROOM.

                              TOM

          He wouldn't do that to us. Not Dr.

          Hartley.

                              BOB

          Well, I'm not doing it to anyone. I

          just . . .

                              MOTHER

          (IN HORROR) You mean it's true?

                              CARLIN

          He's flying to New Orleans tonight.

                              BOB

          I'm leaving you in very capable hands.

                              MOTHER

          You're going . . . out of the state?

                    FATHER

        (TO MOTHER) Of course it's out of the

        state. Where do you think New Orleans

        is, stupid?

                    MOTHER

        Who do you think you're calling stupid,

        liver-lips?

                    TOM

        Dad, you can't let him do this. We

        can't get along without these

        sessions.

                    MOTHER

        I'll tell you what we can get along

        without. Your big mouth!

                    BECKY

        Oh, shut up.

                    FATHER

        Don't sass your mother.

                    BECKY

        I'd rather sass you anyway,

        liver-lips.

THE FAMILY DISSOLVES INTO A BROUHAHA. BOB LOOKS AT
CARLIN.

                    CARLIN

        Now, this is what I call a family.

```
HE EXITS AND WE:


FADE OUT.


END OF ACT ONE
```

Bob, of course, faces more difficulties in act 2. In every scene there are more obstacles to his dramatic need—he can't find his brown suit; they can't get plane tickets at the last minute; when they get tickets, the airport's shut down; Carlin continues to shadow him; and the Swerdlow kids discover their parents were never married and lose it. Just when it appears Bob's a sure candidate for the bunny suit, in a last ditch effort he manages to go on the trip.

7.

WRITING THE HOUR EPISODE

THE HOUR EPISODE, IN MANY ways, is less restrictive than the half-hour sitcom. We are no longer limited to standing sets on a soundstage, or the limited exteriors of a single-camera show. We now have a myriad of locales and visual possibilities. Dexter can go anywhere in Miami to analyze a blood spatter for the Miami Metro Police. Wherever the show takes place becomes your palette for possible locations.

The power of the half-hour comedy rests almost entirely on character and dialogue. The hour episode, while it uses the same hooks, relies on character, dialogue, and the pacing of the visuals—moving pictures to hold the audience.

There are two types of hour TV dramas: series with closure, *procedurals*, where the stories tie up at the end, and *serial dramas*, which have continuing storylines.

Hour serials rely on larger ongoing casts, fewer outside characters, parallel storylines, and fast-paced cutting between elements to grab the audience. These shows include *Brothers and Sisters*, *Grey's Anatomy*, *Heroes*, and *Lost*. *Heroes* and *Lost* are action serials that rely on jeopardy and suspense, but the majority of serials sell characters in conflict. Their storylines are personal and revolve around relationships, the emotions of love, fear, loss, anxiety, sexuality, ambition, infidelity, and, essentially, all the conflicts of human beings. Structuring parallel storylines can be challenging; we will discuss it in Chapter 8.

Hour shows vary in tone but all rely on quick-paced cuts between scenes. Just watch a prime-time hour episode and count how often the locales change. Since we have now expanded into the sixty-minute time frame, our stories become more complex and our costs increase. Unlike in the half-hour comedy, where the action rarely leaves the stars, in the one-hour episode we must cut away from the main characters to reveal the needed layers of more intricate plotting and storytelling.

THE ONE-HOUR STRUCTURE

The classic TV structure for television drama is in four acts. These scripts are about fifty-five to sixty pages, or about one minute per page. On average, each act runs about fourteen or fifteen pages. There are exceptions. Action takes less space than dialogue, so scripts for shows like *The West Wing* with fast-paced dialogue can run up to sixty-five pages.

Many shows have turned to five acts, or five acts with a teaser. These scripts run shorter, coming in at about forty-eight pages and running about eight pages per act, and some six-act shows, like ABC's *Ugly Betty* or *Grey's Anatomy*, can come in even shorter, at about forty-three to forty-five pages. Again, the easiest way to deal with the different formats is to buy episodes from the show and structure your story around the act ends—where the commercials go.

Scene counts on hour shows can go all over the place. I always tell writers that scenes should not run longer than two and a half pages, which equal two and a half minutes in the hour format, or three pages at the very most. Why? Anything longer is stagnant. The writer is relying on dialogue and exposition rather than using visuals and pacing to move the story forward.

Each act in the hour show is a separate unit, with a crisis and a climax all its own. Ask, what must I accomplish in this unit to tell my story? What is the major thrust? The act end is always the climax. It is where the commercial goes and what everything builds toward.

CREATING SUSPENSE

Medical, law, police investigation, and action shows fall under the category of procedurals. These dramas rely on external events to tell their story. The bigger the crisis, the adversary, or the crime, the more powerful the story.

It is crucial that you give your protagonists worthy adversaries. The stronger the antagonists and their M.O. (modus operandi), the better your protagonist looks. We all know the ruthless and relentless cyborg villain in *Terminator 2*, but what about the killer that fascinates Dexter, or the serial rapist toying with Deputy Chief Brenda Johnson's head? What makes these characters tick? What's fascinating about them? Where are their layers? Multidimensional characters are crucial in a spec script. No cookie-cutter, cardboard bad guys; producers hate them!

Character + Dramatic Need + Obstacles + Conflict = Action

The bigger the obstacles, the stronger the conflict, and the more powerful the script. Too often in my script consulting, I've come across scripts that are too convenient on the part of the writer. If you are scripting a story in which an undercover agent has to penetrate a high-security installation, don't let her slip through an open window. Contrivances such as these diminish the power of your hero and destroy the credibility of your script. Writers succumb to this temptation because making it too hard on their heroes means making it too hard on themselves. The trade-off is a sellout and it won't pay off. Push your characters to the limit. If you want to grab your audience, create a dilemma that pushes your protagonist to the edge of a cliff; increase her jeopardy so she hangs on the edge for dear life, throw rocks at her until she has to let go, and don't catch her until the last moment. Not until then does your character, using her (your) cunning and ingenuity, manage to escape.

Nobody said it was easy. When I started writing suspense stories with sophisticated villains, anything Madeline DiMaggio would think of for the investigation simply wasn't good enough. I needed to do hard research and mind gymnastics to come up with something clever and savvy. There were no shortcuts.

The Inferior and Superior Positions of the Audience

Jeopardy and suspense can be constructed in different ways. One is to place your audience in the *superior position*. That is, let them know beforehand what could happen to our hero or heroes. Let's create a scenario. A couple is going camping. We, the writers, establish beforehand that a brutal beast is stalking the area where they are headed. They reach their destination, pitch their camp, then cozily tuck in for the night. The beast approaches in the wee hours. He ravages their campsite, rips them apart, and has them for dinner.

Where have we placed the audience? In the inferior or superior position? The superior, because the audience knows before the campers what is about to happen.

Imagine now that we begin with the campers. We place our audience inside the tent. They hear a noise: something is lurking outside. After an eerie silence, the noise comes again. It approaches the tent. Suddenly, without warning, the hideous presence bursts forth. Here, we have placed the audience in the *inferior position* because they are discovering the beast with the campers. In most one-hour action episodes, the writer can use both points of view. In *Women's Murder Club*, the audience makes its discoveries with Det. Lindsay Boxer, but the writer can still place a killer behind a door lying in wait for her. We see him, but she doesn't as she comes up the stairs. This creates good tension. Always ask yourself which P.O.V. (point of view) delivers the greatest impact.

Another device in creating tension is withholding information. It keeps the audience in the discovery process. I remember being stuck once on a caper script. The producer had me make a list of everything that needed to come out and then go back and "thread" the information. What wasn't I going to let my protagonist know? What did I want to withhold from the audience? What could they discover, but with a piece missing? What would lead to a bigger complication and another question?

On clue-driven shows, many writers start at the end of the story and work backward. If you are writing a spec *House*, it's easier to choose the disease first, then start eliminating everything it's not or mimicking. I asked a writer who once wrote for *Columbo* how they came up with such terrific M.O.'s and wonderful characters. He said that first they chose the objects, then they developed a crime around the objects, and then they developed the character. (We will cover character development in a later chapter.)

THE HOUR SETUP

The hour setup, with the exclusion of some serials, is almost always complete by the third or fourth scene.

The *Starsky and Hutch* episode we discussed earlier opened on the *runner*. Sometimes this is a handy device since your characters must be doing something in time and space. Starsky is trying to get Hutch to invest in one of his get-rich-quick schemes. Hutch isn't buying it. Captain Dolby interrupts them; another body has turned up dead from strychnine poisoning *(B story)*.

At this point the scene was running two and a half pages, so we cut to another locale to keep the action moving. Dolby says, "And there's something else, come into my office."

In *scene 2,* they learn they'll have company when they go

out on the street. C. D. Phelps, a syndicated columnist for the *Tribune*, is going with them. Here we use a handy device called *pointing an arrow*. The question arose that was a possible problem: "Why, out of all the cops in Los Angeles, does this columnist want them?" By pointing a finger at the problem and addressing it, we plugged the credibility issue, eradicating it:

STARSKY
What's he doing with us?!

DOLBY
Writing a two-part article on what he
calls "Counterculture Cops—The New
Breed."

HUTCH
Look, Captain, we've got two possible
homicides . . . Assign him to somebody
else.

DOLBY
He likes your track record; you're the
ones he wants.

Moments later there's a knock at the door and a beautiful woman (*A story*) sticks her head in. The men eye one another, trip over themselves with the introductions, and call Dolby into the hallway, where they say they'd be willing to reconsider. The setup is complete.

Boston Legal combines both procedural (closed) and serialized (ongoing) storylines. The setup always starts on a *cold opening* (the same as a teaser).

In a terrific episode, "Roe v. Wade: The Musical," written

by Susan Dickes and Jill Goldsmith, Missy, Shirley's ex-husband's ex-wife, tells Shirley she's madly in love with a beautiful African American and having his baby. There's one problem—he's suing her because she took his semen without his knowing (*A story*).

In *scene 1*, Leigh, Jerry's former girlfriend, comes to Jerry and asks him to defend her after she's been fired as a teacher for consoling a student with a hug in violation of a zero-tolerance policy for physical contact (*B story*).

Scene 2, the African American, an acquaintance of Alan's, says he cannot live with the terrible woman who practically raped him. He is the son of an absentee father. It's a problem endemic in the African American culture and he will not participate in or contribute to it. Alan has to help him not have this baby.

Scene 3 takes place in the courtroom. Jerry adamantly objects when it's implied that Leigh hugged more than once, and that the hugs were of a sexual nature. He has little recourse when the prosecutor asks her about her recent diagnosis of objectaphilia. "A condition," she explains, "where one is sexually attracted to objects."

In *scene 4*, Shirley is thrown into a stupor when Alan says his client's semen was stolen and they are asking for an abortion. "Has he read a little case called Roe v. Wade?" "Yes," says Alan, "and wouldn't the current Supreme Court just love an opportunity to overthrow Roe without being vilified as anti-abortion." Shirley is too livid at his absurd notion to try to argue this, under the law; Alan has no right whatsoever to get a court-ordered abortion. He knows Shirley and he can tell by the tone in her voice that she is daring him to try it.

By scene 4 the setup is complete. The A story is a great twist—a liberal fighting to override a woman's right to choose, and there's personal involvement for the stars. It's not just Shirley and Alan facing off. It's man against woman.

BUILD TO THE ACT ENDS

All hour scripts build to the act end, regardless of how many acts they include, and they thrive on twists, especially procedurals.

I recently caught a *Cold Case* episode, "Thick as Thieves," written by the show's creator, Meredith Stiehm, and Christopher Silber. The CBS show has five acts and a teaser. Each act held suspense, built to a powerful end, and had a twist:

The *teaser* opens on a beautiful woman entering a country club and asking for a membership. Eighteen years later, in present day, a bag lady is found dead on the Philadelphia streets. She's been shot in the face.

Act 1, we learn the gunshot is from an attempted murder eighteen years earlier, and the woman who we thought was a bag lady has come out of a coma and been living in a vegetative state on the city's dime ever since. Every month someone sent her a gift package of Godiva chocolates, caviar, and champagne. An autopsy shows she has saline implants, circa 1989. Very expensive for that time. At *act 1 end,* Jane Doe, at the time of her attempted murder, was far from being broke, or maybe whoever was taking care of her wanted her out of the way.

Act 2, Jane Doe is identified. A composite photo shows Margo Chambers, a pretty woman in her midthirties, who was shot in the face. There were no witnesses. The saline implants are traced to a plastic surgeon. He remembers Margo; they belonged to the same country club.

In a flashback, Margo, who has had one too many, spots a cabana boy, Spencer, coming on to a woman at the pool. She's livid, exchanges words with him, and throws her drink in his face.

Lilly and Jeffries track down the woman. She confesses to having an affair with Spencer and says Margo was threatening him. They both needed to get away. In a flashback she meets Spencer at a secret place and brings fifty thousand dollars cash. They spot Margo driving toward them in the distance. Spencer jumps in his car and says he'll divert her and that he'll come back. The woman tells Lilly and Jeffries that he never returned. At the *act 2 end,* Lilly gets a crime sheet on Margo's aliases and discovers that she and Spencer were partners.

In *act 3,* the team tracks down Spencer and interrogates him. He says he got tired of the game. In another flashback we see a man coming to their room and threatening Margo for what she did to his brother. With Spencer watching from behind a door, she produces a gun and makes him leave. Spencer tells the officers he hated that he is aware of what they are doing to people and wants out. The day he left he says Margo was running scared. His story matches up. They track the man to the trailer park where Margo grew up. His intentions were never to hurt her; he knew what she was up to and wanted to turn her in. He planted a device (tape recorder) in the room. When he went back for it, they were gone. At *act 3 end,* we learn that Spencer wasn't Margo's boyfriend, he was her son.

In *act 4,* Margo hatches a plan to fake her own death. They can use Spencer's girlfriend; there's enough resemblance. She will sign over her insurance policy to Spencer, and they can leave the country rich and live normal lives like he's always wanted.

The woman at the country club is ID'd at the location of the murder. She's brought in for questioning. She spent weeks tracking Margo and Spencer down. When she pulled up to the motel, she saw Spencer enter a room with a woman. She didn't know who it was. She saw him shoot her. The curtains were drawn, and she heard a second shot and fled.

At the *act 4 end,* they find the insurance policy signed over to Linus Larabee (Spencer) on the day Margo was murdered. Margo, the master grifter, was beaten at her own game.

In *act 5,* Lilly finds Spencer. He says he loved his mother, nobody understood him like she did. All he ever wanted was to be normal. In a flashback, the body of Spencer's girlfriend lies in the motel room. Margo signs the policy, tells Spencer to hurry up. When she turns around, he's pointing the gun at her, and his girlfriend is standing behind him. Margo pleads for her life. Spencer can't pull the trigger. His girlfriend grabs the gun and shoots Margo in the head.

At *show end,* Spencer's girlfriend confesses to the shooting. In a flashback she goes to the hospital where Spencer stands by his mother who is in a coma. His girlfriend can't convince him to leave. She looks at Margo, who once again has won. One side of Margo's face is bandaged, but one eye stares eerily back at the girl.

If you look at the example of *Cold Case,* each act is synopsized by what needs to happen to move the story forward, and each act end is identified.

In developing the hour script, start with the broad overview and identify the end or destination point first. Starting with the big picture is always easier. Once you know where you are headed you can then go back and step out the scenes you need to get you there. It's like following a road map.

We will explore this more fully in Chapter 8.

8.

DEVELOPING AN EPISODE
STEP BY STEP

WE HAVE LEARNED THE TOOLS of television writing, the hooks of the medium, and the act structures of the half-hour and one-hour episodes. Now how can we apply what we've learned? When do we know we're ready to begin?

First, you must study the show you choose to write for—watch it, rewatch it, and read scripts from the show. If it's a half hour, is it a single-camera show or three-camera show? If it's an hour show, is it in four acts, five acts with a teaser, or six acts? Know the characters thoroughly!

Next, don't settle on just any idea. Take time to come up with something clever, innovative, and not derivative of anything that has aired on that show before. A way to check on this is to go onto imdb.com and enter the show's name. In the left column hit the episode list and it will give you the log lines of the shows that have previously aired.

I am often asked: How does a writer develop an idea? What is the writer's process? Instead of theorizing, it is better to walk you through one of my own scripts. I'm using a half-hour show simply because the structure is smaller and faster. It is important to note that the process is the same for the half-hour show, the one-hour show, or the two-hour movie. Most of us have caught reruns of *Three's Company*. If you haven't, it was about two single girls and a single guy sharing an apartment in Santa Monica, California.

I knew what the show sold—T and A (tits and ass), cohabitation, and great physical comedy by the late John Ritter. In searching for an idea I turned to myself first, maybe there was a nugget there, if it was happening to me maybe it could be happening to one of them.

I recalled a law student I had met three years earlier. We went out on a perfect date. We never ran out of things to talk about. I sensed that this was the beginning of something special. I waited by the phone, but I never heard from him.

A year later, when I had finally forgotten about him he called me. He apologized and explained he did not pass the bar and got bogged down with his studies and a move. His excuse sounded legitimate, so I accepted another date. I waited by the phone and again he didn't call. A year later I got another call and he asked me out again! Always, the creep would disappear for a year and then pop up again! He was the last person in the world I ever wanted to see.

I asked myself—Could this experience be a springboard (something that provides an idea) for *Three's Company*? Was it identifiable to the masses? Was there something in it that viewers could relate to? Yes, because it deals with rejection—who at some time has not been rejected?

At this point the writer begins asking questions so that he or she can come up with the appropriate answers. Whose story must it be? Jack's, Janet's, or Chrissy's? Actually, this story could happen to any one of them since the show sold three stars.

I decided it would be Jack's story. I now had a log line.

STEP 1: The log line conveys the premise of the episode in one or two lines: An old paramour of Jack's returns and makes him fall head over heels all over again.

The writer continues to ask questions to flesh out the story. Who is the lady who pops in and out of his life? What should she do for a living? If she can come and go on a whim maybe she works for the airlines. Will we want to like her? How should the story end? Weigh the possibilities—what works best for you? Writing is making choices—and the more interesting the choices, the better the script.

The same process is used for the hour script. The log line for the *Cold Case* episode we looked at in Chapter 7 would read something like this: Detectives try to solve the case of a woman who comes out of a coma and dies from a shot to the head eighteen years earlier.

STEP 2: Identify the thrust of the act. Look at each act as a separate unit. Write a very brief summation of what needs to happen to move the story forward.

STEP 3: Identify each act end.

STEP 4: Look at what you've got so far. Can your story be set up, developed, and resolved in the half-hour or one-hour time frame? Is there a good hook? Can there be a quick setup? Is your star pivitol to the story? Who is driving the action? Is there personal involvement for the characters?

STEP 5: Use the same process developing the B story.

STEP 6: If what you have works, go back and begin stepping out (breaking down) the scenes. You already know what has to be revealed and your act end. Now, the question is, How do you get there?

Stepping out the scenes is crucial in structuring the teleplay. Index cards are handy for this.

When you are done with an act, put your inner critic to work. Ask yourself, is there a strong enough build? Does each scene move the story forward? Is there enough conflict for the characters? Did I place enough obstacles in their paths? Should I change the order of the scenes? Is there a big enough cliffhanger? Do it with each of the acts and then with the piece as a whole. Is there continuity? Does the story flow?

Before going to first draft and writing in script format, there is another step which is very helpful. I call it the *interior voice* (see Chapter 12).

SERIALS AND PARALLEL STORYLINES

Unlike the procedurals, serials and parallel storylines cannot be defined with a brief summary for each act. The writer is juggling too many storylines with no idea at first where they will land. Here's how to proceed:

- First, you must know the show extremely well.

- Watch the show and study it over and over. Jot down the storylines in each act. How many are there? What is the order of their importance? Where do they fall into the acts?

- Buy episodes of the script and break them down. You usually can't specify an episode when you buy these scripts, but the formats are the same. For example, *Brothers and Sisters* is in six acts, with usually five running parallel storylines: stories A, B, C, D, and E. In the setup, the A, B, C, and sometimes D story are almost always established.

- Begin with a simple log line for the first storyline. Example: A romance between Nora and Isaac develops. Take it no further than three scenes— beginning, middle, and end. Nora's upset; Isaac hasn't contacted her since the disastrous family dinner. On Kitty's advice, she asks him to lunch. He can't go but invites her to dinner instead. They both realize something very special is happening.

- Use the same process on all of the stories.

- Get out index cards, corkboards, pushpins, or anything else that will help you track the storylines. Lay the cards down in acts (beginning, middle, and end). See how it lays out.

- The A story will probably expand to five scenes, the B and C story to four, and the D story to three. Just play around with them and see what works.

Another great way to study parallel storylines is to photo-copy the script of an episode, cut and paste each story together as a whole unit and study them. See how long they run, how they are developed, and where the writer chose to cut.

Writing nonlinear material is challenging, but also a lot of fun, and when you are analyzing the writing on these shows, you'll be learning from the best.

There are exceptions to everything I tell you.

Showrunner Kevin Falls said, when working on *The West Wing* for creator/writer/executive producer Aaron Sorkin, that Sorkin would not allow the words "A, B, C, and D stories" in the writers' room. Sorkin broke all the rules of television. If he wanted to start a story in act 3 and resolve it by act 4, he pulled it off.

If you can write like Aaron Sorkin or David E. Kelley, you don't need this book, you can do anything you want. Go write.

9.

HOW TO CREATE RIVETING CHARACTERS

STRUCTURE HOLDS THE STORY IN place, but it is character, scene by scene, line by line, that takes you through the script. In writing episodic television, it is your job to know the characters. In writing pilots and movies for television and cable, it is your job to create them.

Once you have determined the spine, time frame, and turning points of your story, your characters, if fully developed, will tell you where to go. I like to illustrate this by sharing a personal horror story.

My partner and I had been successful in episodic TV for a number of years, when a producer, the late Phil Mandelker, called us in to develop our first movie of the week.

The springboard was a soapy tour de force for two female leads, with possible series potential (a backdoor pilot). The characters grew up together and, after a long separation, meet again. One is a very successful executive, and the other is trying to keep afloat. They find themselves locked in a situation with the same man, and it triggers an explosion of old conflicts.

He gave brief sketches of the characters; we bounced around thoughts and were told to go home and develop them further. We were to start with Sharon, the high-powered executive.

Having had experience only in episodic television, where characters for the most part are already established, we developed some pages and brought them back to Phil. I will never forget sitting in his office watching him read them. After a few moments, he looked up at me and asked, "Do you call this writing?"

It was one of those terrible moments you never forget. I wanted to jump off his balcony, but I was afraid anything that theatrical would go unnoticed on the Warner Bros. lot, and then I would not only be humiliated, I would be dead.

Moments like these only have usefulness if you don't repeat them, and I'm glad to say I haven't.

Instead of cutting us off (writers' jargon for firing), Phil had us meet at his home, where for the next two weeks we developed our characters. We began with Sharon's back life, but that was only the beginning.

A CHARACTER'S BACK LIFE/ PRESENT LIFE

Sharon's *back life* was everything of consequence that had taken place in her life before the film began. Who were her parents? How much money did they have? Where did they live? Did she compete with her brother or sister? Was she popular in school? Did she struggle with her grades, or did they come easily to her?

Phil asked, "When was her first sexual experience? How was she perceived by the opposite sex? Who were her friends in the neighborhood? What side of the tracks did she live on? What church did she go to?" And on and on he went. And on and on.

I eyed my partner, and she eyed me back. The detail was getting a little absurd. There was no way in hell we were going to fit this into two hours. I failed to see that knowing how much money Sharon's parents had in the bank when she was born would have any effect on our script, but we went along with Phil anyway. After all, he was the producer and we were the writers, and we weren't stupid. If nothing else came out of this, at least we were making a good contact, even if this guy was a little strange.

The sessions continued and we turned to Sharon's present life.

The *present life* includes everything of significance about the character once the film begins. There are only three ways to reveal characters in film—by their professional, personal, and private moments, and Phil had us pursue each of these with the same diligence and detail.

A strange thing was beginning to happen. I started getting caught up in these sessions and looking forward to them. I found myself thinking about Sharon a lot. On my long commute home to Westlake Village, I'd wonder how Sharon would react and relate to other characters in the script. I even wondered how she would relate to people in my own life! It was as though she was beginning to exist on some invisible plane.

I thought about her abusive father and the alcoholic mother

who was resigned to living with him, the humiliation her parents had caused her in school, her early sexual promiscuity, the skeletons in her closet, and the talent and physical assets she used to climb the corporate ladder. I was getting to know her like you would an intimate friend. I could write pages on her years growing up. I knew the defining moments that had changed her life. I even knew her favorite color.

One day Phil asked me, "What does her office look like?"

I said, "It's exquisite!"

He bellowed, "What the hell is *exquisite*?"

I jumped, completely intimidated. Suddenly, I was being made to think like a filmmaker! He was forcing me to think visually.

The office no longer was just exquisite. It became marble and muted pastels, Renoir sketches, a Louis XIV desk, and decor audacious enough to compete with the city skyline. It was eccentric and exceedingly feminine, like the president who occupied it.

Suddenly pictures started coming into my mind. The pictures became locales. The people in Sharon's life started popping up, and they become the characters in the movie!

We were not conscious of it yet, but as we were developing our characters, we were actually developing our story!

The project, entitled *California Reunion*, never got the green light, but it was one of my favorite projects, and an invaluable experience—one that would serve me well when seven years later I had a classic case of burnout and my life was falling apart like one of our own characters.

. . .

My partner and I went on to many other projects. We worked nonstop. If I wasn't writing, I was thinking about writing. There was never a day off. I tried a trip to Europe with my husband once, but I was called back by an executive for rewrites on a pilot. The negatives of the profession started to get to me: the pressures of deadlines, having little or no control over my own material, and working with demanding executives, whom I was too timid to challenge. Instead of excitedly anticipating the next job, I secretly began dreading it, knowing how much work was involved. The relationship with my partner was becoming increasingly more difficult, and the stress was beginning to affect the quality of our work.

The money that I had earned in television up to this point had been invested in my husband's business. Now the company, which initially had done well, was on the verge of financial collapse. I remembered once going to a meditation master who asked me what I wanted. I told him spiritual awareness. I was hoping this wasn't it. If it was, I wanted to take back my request.

A year later, I arrived on the Monterey Peninsula divorced, bankrupt, split from my writing partner, and a single parent.

One day a friend asked me to speak to his college writing class, and so began my five-year stint with teaching. For a while it was very satisfying, but the more I talked about writing screenplays, the more I missed it. I missed the industry, the pitching sessions, and the adrenaline rush of driving onto the studio lot. I missed seeing my name on the television screen, and quite honestly, I missed the lucrative income. But most of all I missed the writing.

I wanted to go for it again. But how? I hadn't had a credit

in years. Once I left Hollywood, I foolishly made no attempts to keep in touch with my contacts. I no longer even had an agent. It would be like starting all over. I had to write a spec script. I had no idea what to write about. And then it hit me.

I went to work on a comedy based on my experiences in bankruptcy. Write what you know . . . I entitled the script *Belly Up*, and used the same process for developing my protagonist, Alex Holman, that Phil had taught us in *California Reunion.*

I went to work on Alex's back story. I decided he did not come from money, yet things still seemed to come easily to him. He was attractive and bright, and he never had to stretch too far. He went to Stanford on a student loan. While there, he met Jerry Weiner, an idealistic premed student who had visions of becoming a reconstructive plastic surgeon. One day he would perform microsurgery on burn victims, climb the Himalayas, and go into remote villages and work with lepers.

At the top of the script, Jerry has instead become a very successful Beverly Hills plastic surgeon. He drives a Ferrari and has a model trophy wife. His posh office looks like a war zone, filled with too many bandages, liposuctions, and implants. He's managed to get to the Himalayas once, not out of guilt, but because he said he would. He likes the amenities that success has afforded him.

Act 2 of the movie opens at Harry's Bar and Grill. Alex has just gone bankrupt, and Jerry's wife has left him. They're drinking martinis and commiserating as they line up the olives, reminiscing about the old days at Stanford, when they used to bronze their jockstraps and send them to the sorority housemothers. This scene grew out of the back life I'd developed for Alex.

While at Stanford, I decided, Alex had met his wife, Felicia. She came from money; this is not why he married her, but it's very typical of the kind of woman he would be drawn to. Felicia was happily ensconced in California's Bay Area society when Alex decided to relocate his wife and daughter, Brooke, to Los Angeles.

Later, in bankruptcy court, the spoiled former debutante has a complete breakdown. She can't afford a personal trainer or filler for her lips, and now she's got athlete's foot because she's had to join a public gym. She screams, "You son of a bitch! I never wanted to leave Palo Alto!" Where did the dialogue come from? It came from the back life of Alex's character.

I decided that when Alex relocated to Los Angeles, he had gone to work for two very conservative Jewish land developers named Haberman and Hern. Alex's "hotdog" enthusiasm and innovative ideas had proved a shot in the arm for the company. He'd made them a fortune, and in return, they called him "the goy wonder."

When the movie opens, Hern is dead: he had keeled over from a heart attack three months earlier. A black wreath is still hanging on his door. Haberman, faced with his own mortality, has totally flipped. He keeps a picture of his deceased partner on an empty conference room chair and talks to him in business meetings.

He is also trying to have sex with every temp girl who comes through the office. Haberman needs sex to feel alive. Needless to say, his volatile condition has left investors nervous, and Alex has the sole responsibility of trying to hold the company together.

In developing the back life of Alex, I now had four secondary characters for my movie: Jerry Weiner, the frustrated plastic surgeon; Felicia, the spoiled wife; Brooke, his indulged adolescent daughter; and Sidney Haberman, the neurotic partner.

Alex took financial chances. His philosophy was that life is a gamble, and he is a winner. It occurred to me that a man with this attitude could make some pretty heavy wagers on the golf course. Early in the script, he wins a thousand-dollar bet.

Later, he not only loses his five-thousand-dollar Rolex thanks to a missed putt, but he must also run naked to the parking lot, where the cops spot him and arrest him for indecent exposure.

With Alex's back life complete, my focus turned to the present: my character's professional life, his personal life, and his private life.

PROFESSIONAL LIFE

A character's professional life is more than an office or a title. It is a series of moving pictures, not just one locale. It is a routine. It becomes his alarm clock, what he eats for breakfast, the building he lives in, the Starbucks he habitually pulls into, the way he orders his latte, and the route he drives to work.

When your character arrives at the office, is there a space reserved for him in a subterranean parking lot? Is there a doorman who greets him? On what floor is his office? When he steps off the elevator, how wide is the hallway? When he reaches the office, what does the doorman say? Inside, how many secretaries are at work? How many phones are ringing? What do the pictures on the walls reveal?

I needed to establish that Alex was in land development. The challenge for the scriptwriter is always how to show instead of talk about. So I decided to have photographs in the outer office of the company's various developments: the three partners cutting a ribbon in front of a new supermarket, photographs of bulldozers clearing land, a photograph of a landfill, with Alex in a hardhat. Each picture revealed more about the company. In the corner of the room is a scale model of a current housing development named Holman Hills.

Who is your character's secretary? What is their relationship? Is it business? Are they best of friends, or is it more intimate? Who are your characters' partners and who do they work with? Remember, these people are the possible characters in your script. Who comes in, who goes out? See it in your head.

PERSONAL LIFE

A character's personal life is everything that is not professional or private. Just think of your own personal life. Who are the people in it? How do you interact socially? What are your hobbies? Where do you hang out? What does your personal world look like?

Let's begin with the family. Is your character married? Who is he married to? What is the interaction between them? What do they talk about? Is their sex life spontaneous, or do they only consider making love on the weekends? We have all been to parties and in social situations where we have seen couples who are outwardly pleasant, caring, and even loving, and yet there is an obvious unspoken tension between them. What are they hiding? What do they show to the world, and what do they show to each other?

We have also seen couples who bat words back and forth, tease, and give each other a rough time, and yet there is a sense of underlying love beneath these behaviors. There is a group consciousness and there is a couple consciousnesses, a dialogue, a routine, a pattern of interaction that is as unique as the partners participating. Nowhere else can we push each other's buttons as we can in intimate relationships.

What are your character's "buttons"? How about children? Do they have any? What are the kids like? How do the parents interact with them; what roles do they play? Playmate? Friend? How do the children deal with their parents? Are the kids up front, or are they forced to sneak around their parents?

Alex has a daughter, Brooke. She is fourteen, ghetto chic, bright, and definitely her own person. Her obsession is with photography. She takes still photographs of inanimate objects, like an apple, from twenty different angles, and she's a genius at covering up new tattoos. Although they love each other, Dad's her ATM. This will change when Alex goes broke and only has time to give. That's when they get to know each other.

Identify your characters' relationships and the ways they will change over the course of the story.

Into the personal life of the character come friends. Who are they? With whom has your character chosen to associate? In college, Alex Holman chose Jerry Weiner. They were very different. Alex wanted material things. Jerry was esoteric and idealistic. What was their bond? Youth, Stanford, and women. In present life, they flip-flop. Jerry has completely bought into the material world and the stress that goes along with it. Alex will lose his possessions and must now search for something more meaningful.

PRIVATE LIFE

What do your characters do when no one is watching? Who are they when they are completely alone? Private moments are a peek into a character's soul.

In *About Schmidt*, superbly crafted by screenwriters Alexander Payne and Jim Taylor, Schmidt's character, played by Jack Nicholson, is so layered, so vacant, so deprived of his own potential that you ache for him. You might say it's the brilliance of Jack Nicholson that makes Schmidt, but it was the character of Schmidt that brought the genius of Jack Nicholson on board to want to play him.

This film is filled with private moments. We watch Schmidt through the difficult ritual of retirement, struggling with a lack of self-esteem, a lack of purpose, and trying to find a reason to get up in the morning. And then we watch him as a widower forced to face this new phase of his life alone. We laugh at him, we cry with him, and we dread becoming like him. No matter what our circumstances are in life, we identify with this character's futility and humanity.

The movie opens on a private moment. Schmidt, in a cleaned-out, no-window office, sits looking up at the clock as the second hand counts down the seconds until his retirement. With each tick we sense his life slipping away, we feel his dread.

When the clock strikes, he gets up, looks around one last time, then shuts the door. It is a beautiful metaphor.

Tony Soprano was a brutal mob boss filled with many contradictions. He loved his wife but cheated on her relentlessly. He could easily lie, but he also kept his word. He let no one offend or hurt his children and was secretly haunted by the fear that A. J., his son, carried his family curse. He struggled at times with a conscience, or so it appeared, and he sought help. As a boy he had been emotionally damaged, and there were times he could be gentle.

I was hoping there might be some humanity that could be resurrected in Tony. In a private moment, in season 6, in the episode entitled "Kennedy and Heidi," Tony kills his nephew Christopher. They are in a terrible car accident on a desolate road. Christopher is seriously hurt and Tony takes advantage of the fact. Christopher has fallen off the wagon and become a liability, so Tony clamps his hand over Chris's nose and mouth and smothers him to death. His eyes are like a predator's, lifeless and flat. The act was done with so much ease that I knew I was wrong about him. The scene sent shivers down my spine.

One of the best screenplay dramas ever written is the Academy Award–winning *Ordinary People*, adapted for the screen by Alvin Sargent. In it, Sargent gives us a "window" into the mother's soul through a sequence of private moments. In one, Beth comes through the front door and Sargent comments on her perfect body. She walks into her very neat, organized kitchen and opens the refrigerator and looks inside.

There is a close-up of the interior, and we can tell by the

description of the contents that it is a metaphor for Beth: cold, sparse, evenly distributed, and perfectly covered with Saran Wrap. She closes the refrigerator door, then takes a stack of towels from the service porch and walks up a flight of stairs. At the top of the stairs she notices a plant stand. It is crooked, so she moves it just slightly to the right.

Next she goes into the bedroom and puts the towels away. Then, Sargent writes, "Something occurs to Beth." She walks to her perfect desk, removes a perfect pencil, and jots down a note. There is a close-up on the note that reads, *Don't forget the Johnsons' Xmas.*

This woman is so consumed with appearances that later in the script her husband comments that she asked what he would wear to their own son's funeral.

The first time we meet Rocky Balboa, he returns home after sparring in the ring. In his rundown apartment an old mattress serves as a makeshift punching bag. He takes his pet turtle and places its bowl next to the bowl of his pet fish, Moby Dick, so they can keep each other company. We can sense his loneliness.

At the mirror, he looks at his bruised and battered face. Nearby is a picture of himself as a child—innocent and untarnished. He looks at the picture, then back into the mirror. Resigned, he grabs ice from the fridge, places it on his bruises, and flops dejectedly on his bed. In this private moment our hearts go out to this man. We're won over. We're rooting for him the rest of the movie.

In *Lars and the Real Girl*, Nancy Oliver paints Lars as an emotionally wounded young man who lives in a garage apartment behind his brother's house. We first meet Lars dressed for church, looking out the window, obviously set apart from the world. His room is austere; there is one cup and one plate, and old furniture he's had since he was a kid. At church, we see he's a kind soul, always doing things for people. They like him, but he's painfully shy and awkward. Alone that night, in his garage apartment, Oliver has Lars sitting on his bed in the dark. He's still in his church clothes; it's 4 a.m. He hasn't moved. He's been awake all night. Later, when Lars goes to the mall, he wanders aimlessly and sees nothing but families and couples at the food court. Oliver writes: "He feels his isolation like a physical illness."

THE COMPELLING CHARACTERISTIC

Now you have all this information about your character—his back life and his present life, in all its professional, personal, and private moments. How can you take this information and translate it to film? For this purpose we turn to the compelling characteristic.

Think about your character. Ask yourself which characteristic is the most dominant or profound. What single trait drives him the most? At first, this process may seem highly simplistic. You may feel that in focusing on only one compelling characteristic, you make your character appear one-dimensional.

It sounds simplistic, but this strategy enables the writer to stay on track! It does not mean your character is one-dimensional; it means that out of all their layers, there is one dominant one that drives them, and you play it for all it's worth.

For Schmidt, his compelling characteristic was the need to find some kind of meaning in his life. When he loses both his job and his wife, he takes it upon himself to drive to Denver and stop his daughter from marrying the wrong man. He wants to matter. He wants to know before he dies that he's made a difference in someone's life, that his existence had purpose. This need drives him throughout the film.

For Beth Jarrett in *Ordinary People*, the compelling characteristic is her perfectionism. Her compulsion is constantly crafted throughout the screenplay by Alvin Sargent. Beth's body is perfect, and so is the way she runs her house. Everything is in order. Even the plant stand must be moved just slightly, so that it too is perfect. Beth shows little emotion: emotion is messy and wouldn't live up to her standards.

Though Conrad, her son, is having severe emotional problems, Beth prefers that he not see a psychiatrist. She also refuses family counseling, which could expose her as a not-so-perfect mother. Conrad finally comes to terms with his guilt and grief over his brother's boating accident. So does his father. But growth can be unpleasant and painful, and so, in the end, it is Beth, totally incapable of change, who leaves.

Rocky's compelling characteristic is his compassion. Writer Sylvester Stallone plays it out in almost every scene. Rocky pulls winos off the street, tells hookers to go home, and stops and talks to orphaned animals in pet shops. He strategically places his turtle and goldfish bowls together so the two can keep each other company. Employed as a strong arm for a numbers runner, Rocky gives the client another chance. He finds a very plain woman beautiful and doesn't even dislike his adversary, Apollo Creed. Who wouldn't be rooting for this character? We care so much for him that in the last ten minutes we want to get inside the ring with him and help him out.

Lars wants more than anything to be normal. His desire is so strong that he buys a doll and unknowingly creates a delusional relationship so he can heal himself.

I pondered Alex Holman's compelling characteristic for quite a while. The very thing that motivated Alex, that had brought him success and was the source of his downfall, was his hubris.

Alex's perception of himself and his world is that life is a gamble and that he is a winner. I played with this attitude throughout the script: Alex the winner is now a loser. He could always do the big things well, but that's because everybody else took care of the small stuff. People paid his bills, did his laundry, and even lined up his appointments. All he had to do was make money. Now he can't. He's stuck with the small stuff, like doing his own laundry. He's a big leaguer stuck in Little League. Alex's compelling characteristic created all the humor in the script. I played it out at every opportunity.

As you write, review your character work periodically; things will start jumping out at you. Ideas will pop into your head. Dialogue will come. It will all pay off.

I am often asked by writers how much character work is necessary for secondary and minor cast members. Once you do the work on your main protagonist/protagonists, a lot of work on the rest of the script is already done. I knew Jerry Weiner and Felicia and Alex's partner from Alex's bio.

Minor characters will require much less work, but you can use the compelling characteristic, even for bit parts or walk-ons. It is a wonderful way to give a character a point of view and an attitude.

10.

THE TELEVISION PILOT

I AM APPROACHED ALL THE time by new writers who say they have a great idea for a television series. It is highly unlikely that an unknown writer without a track record can break into the industry with a pilot spec script and get it on the air, no matter how good it is.

The good news is, agents and producers today are more open to reading spec pilots as samples from new writers, to spot innovative and original voices. If you are willing to write a spec pilot to show yourself off creatively, then go for it. But I warn all who attempt it, pulling it off is a daunting task, even for the most experienced of writers. If you feel you can create a "new world," some kind of interesting hook or format, establish compelling characters with unique voices, write it without obvious exposition given the terrific time limitations and prove your franchise has "legs," you're either delusional and have great chutzpah or you're extraordinarily talented, either of which will serve you in this business.

If you are looking at Las Vegas odds, I feel the writer's best shot is writing a backdoor pilot—that is, a movie script that has the potential for a good series. When writing the script, you can't be too obvious with this—let the potential buyers discover the TV potential themselves or else the read will turn them off.

With a backdoor pilot you can market your material two ways. Movies are a lot easier to get read than spec pilots. Let your agent or the producers repping your material know your intentions, and let them handle it as they see fit. There have been rare cases when a new writer has had a successful movie, a series was made from that movie, and the writer was able to bypass the traditional pilot ladder. If Hollywood smells money, all rules are broken. If something terrific can find its way inside, and it gets pushed up the ladder to a network executive who wants it, the network will attach a showrunner to shepherd the project. The original writer will get some kind of credit, and if the show goes, the showrunner will hire experienced writers to staff it.

THE PILOT CONCEPT

When I met with Kevin Falls, we talked about his show *Journeyman*. I asked, Where do his ideas start? Does he begin with a character, or with the "world"? He said the world. He loves going where he's never been before, working in an unusual setting or anyplace that yields compelling stories and rich characters.

The world he created in *Journeyman* was not like any I had seen in sci-fi before. There was a wholly realistic feel to it. The characters far outweighed the device of time travel, and much of the conflict weighed heavily on family. Dan Vassar, the protagonist, moved between time and place trying to make sense of what was happening to him, and the audience was caught up in the discovery with him. There was always the element of the unknown.

When my partner and I were under contract in series development, we did a lot of pitching at the major networks. Always, we opened on our concept—the two- or three-line sales pitch. We followed this by briefly discussing the world, that is, what set this idea apart—its tone, its message, its broad appeal.

What makes a concept work? It is *characters*. Characters breathe life into the concept and provide the necessary conflict that gives the series its ongoing potential. What's the concept of *ER* or *Grey's Anatomy* or *The Practice* or *Boston Legal*? Character only.

Why is it we so often see the most unlikely types thrown together: the ex-judge and the ex-con; the character who goes by the book, and the partner who can't; the man and woman who are attracted to each other but can never quite get together? Be it in the family arena, the work arena, or the battle between the sexes, good characters with big conflicts mean unlimited storylines and therefore the possibility of a long-running show. We saw it in *Friends*. Character works. It will always work, one camera or twelve.

One of the comedy pilots my partner and I developed was *Common Ground*. At the time, interest rates in the country were going up so fast that young couples were trying to grab up condos for 10 percent down, for fear that if they didn't, they'd never own anything. I kept thinking to myself that somewhere in this national predicament there was a timely concept for a television series. Besides God and apple pie, what is more a part of the American dream than living off credit cards and owning your own home?

The pilot concept focused on three working, childless couples in their twenties who were chasing the good life even if it killed them. These three couples had a past together. Some had gone to the same college. Two of the wives were best friends growing up. One had even dated the other's husband. The entire concept of the pilot rested on who lived inside those walls. Who were those couples?

FILLING IN THE CONCEPT

There are two ways to develop characters, one from scratch, as we covered in the last chapter. The other is from a composite of the people we already know, which is great fun. Sometimes the human imagination cannot manufacture anything better than the real thing. I asked myself who I could place in the first condo.

Who did I know, out of many friends, acquaintances, and family, who had dominant, fun characteristics I could work with to exaggerate and intensify? My brother came to mind. At eight, he had decided he wanted to become a millionaire. He subscribed to the *Wall Street Journal* when most kids were reading comic books. He used to borrow our parents' car, take it to the car wash, and get excited when tipping the attendants.

His first bottle of wine was Château Lafite Rothschild. My father almost choked when he discovered how much my brother had paid for it. One of my brother's first jobs was as a caddie at a Southern California country club, where later he became the youngest member and got his golfing buddies to invest in his first project.

In all fairness to my brother, there are many more aspects to his personality than this very one-sided view I have just given you. He is a spiritual person, a devoted father, and he has grown significantly, but let's face it, what's fun about that?

The goal of the writer is not to copy a person. It is rather to find a particular trait or traits that can be exaggerated in creating a character. Using my brother as the prototype, my partner and I created a character named Tony Berman.

Tony Berman is a real estate agent who looks, feels, thinks, and acts successful. He's got everything but the money to back him up—a fancy car, a country club membership, and more. He feels these "toys" are necessary for business, but actually that's his excuse to take his wonderful rewards now.

Tony is slightly naïve when it comes to people; he will always look for justice and is often an arbitrator because of his gifted tongue. The more insecure he is in a situation, the more he relies on his verbiage. He's impulsive and too often tests his own luck.

A follower of Tony Robbins and other positive peers, Tony has a philosophy: if you believe in it hard enough, it'll happen. He believes life's a gamble but he's a winner. Tony's sure success will happen for him. Why not? He's ethical, and anyone with his integrity has got to have God on his side.

Having placed Tony Berman in the first condo, we thought about who to place next door to him. Tony would be only as good as the character we could put him up against.

Who was Berman's antithesis? What character could we place in the second condo who would present the greatest conflict? Who would prove his greatest foil? A friend of mine had the qualities opposite to Berman's. He always played by the rules, didn't believe in shortcuts, and in school consistently made the dean's list. Not once did he overstep his bounds. He graduated with honors from UCLA, found a wonderful wife who wanted to be a homemaker, bought a little house, and then bigger ones. Here was a wonderful character because he represented the opposite of Berman's philosophy. One was "Go for it; life is a gamble," and the other was "Don't rock the boat; play by the rules and you'll get there." Can you imagine the conflict between these two characters and the limitless storylines they could provide?

Again, we only used my friend as a prototype. The writer's job is to create a bigger-than-life person. We named him Michael Kellegrew.

Michael Kellegrew is an attorney. A little wheel in a large firm for the last six years, he is perhaps the brightest member of the three couples. Knowledgeable in even the most obscure subjects, he is not a braggart, abhors risk, is very low-key and matter-of-fact.

Kellegrew deals best with issues in clear-cut black and white, feels he owes it to you to tell you the dismal truth, and could talk endlessly on the inequities of life.

While driving through Beverly Hills, instead of admiring the houses, he wonders how many of the residents are involved in lawsuits. His idea of good reading is "How to Get Through the Oncoming Recession."

Now that we had two conflicting characters, we went to work creating the character who lives in the third condo. What kind of person would drive both Berman and Kellegrew crazy? We couldn't think of anyone we knew, so we created a character from scratch. He's the kind of guy who doesn't care if he ever sees Europe. No stress, no sweat. We named him Jim Owen.

Jim Owen is not as intellectual as Mike, or as intuitive as Tony, but probably the most sensitive of the three. Jim studied engineering for two years, then discovered he could make as much money hanging drywall. Who needed ulcers, angina at forty, or getting laid off? He's politically aware but prefers a Hollywood blockbuster to the six o'clock news. His contentment with life could drive an ambitious soul to drink, but Jim feels, who needs motivation when you've got a good union? He makes more money than either of his neighbors and doesn't understand why it pisses them off. He's incapable of airs, keeps friends from all walks of life, and on occasion brings his street buddies home.

We began matching up our characters with prospective mates. For Berman, we needed a woman who completely reacted against his extravagance, the kind who goes to "Cost-less," buys cheap booze, and puts it in expensive bottles. She is certain her husband's risk taking will someday ruin them.

Chris Berman is curvy, wide-eyed, and exuberant, and she looks at every new experience as an adventure. A top saleswoman in her field, she's secure in her work but not in her personal life. Blunt to a fault and incapable of holding a grudge, she blurts before she thinks, lacking tact and certainly forethought.

Chris will always have her umbrella waiting for a rainy day. Her husband's excessive spending and prolific generosity have taught her to stash grocery money. Her secret bank account attests to the fact that no man is ever going to leave her high and dry. Hysterical outbursts and routine fights are a part of this woman's foreplay.

For Kellegrew, we needed a woman who was constantly frustrated by his overly cautious nature, a lady who wants to have fun, an instigator with a little bit of the devil in her.

Lynda Kellegrew doesn't want to work, but she wants "things" and is not beyond pushing Mike to get them. She's fun-loving, extremely social, and outwardly she possesses a great disposition, but when alone with Mike, she goads him to loosen up and be more like his friends. Why can't he let go? Why can't they have more fun? Why can't he be more like Tony Berman? Lynda looks innocent and angelic, but her former escapades, which few know about, would make you blush.

In the third condo, we matched our hardhat with a princess. They are the only couple who aren't married. And they have a physical relationship that shakes the foundation of the complex.

> *Lori Daniels is intelligent but not ambitious. She's held a multitude of jobs and at the moment is an instructor at a local gym. Her parents, who sent her to USC, wanted her to marry well. Jim isn't exactly what they had in mind, but she moved in with him anyway. She has no complaints, they have great fun, there's an electric attraction between them, and as she often says, "Jimmy doesn't brown-bag it in bed."*

After developing these couples, we added two secondary characters: a maid with a big mouth who works from condo to condo and a biker and former Hell's Angel as grounds keeper. We then went to work identifying the standing sets, the format of the show, and finished with a list of 7 to 8 TV log lines. What we had created was called the Pilot Bible.

We sold *Common Ground* to NBC. It was the characters that sold this project. They made the concept come alive. They made the concept work.

TREATMENTS

A treatment is a synopsis of the storyline told from beginning to end in narrative prose. It can be long or short and serve different purposes. There was a time when treatments were used for selling projects; that is very rare today, though there are exceptions that we will cover. I still find treatments useful for a number of reasons:

A Working Writer's Treatment

We were raised reading narrative prose and we're all comfortable with it. Script formatting is an odd beast. By the time we're formatting, we've reached an editing stage without being conscious of it. We're looking at what our script *looks like,* and when that happens, gems are lost. I've found it very helpful to write out in prose what you see in the scene or what you'd like to accomplish, before you attack the script. The process loosens you up and ideas begin to flow. Whenever I'm stuck, I still turn to treatment writing.

Testing the Market (Short Treatment/Synopsis)

I'll write two or three pages on an idea and test it out on people, especially industry people like indie producers I know. If they don't feel there's a market for it, I'll file it away for another time. Someday you may return to it and it could really spark something, or it'll be exactly what somebody is looking for. Always file your ideas away.

The Treatment for a Sale

These run much longer, perhaps eight to twenty-five pages, and I only write them when it's a better gamble than writing a spec script. A case in point:

My significant other has worked at NASA for many years both as a flight surgeon and an MD to employees, including the astronaut corps and their families. He is a friend of Commander Jon Clark, whose wife, Commander Laurel Clark, was one of the astronauts who perished in the Columbia disaster. Jon gave me the rights to Laurel's life story. It's fascinating. So was their marriage. They were accomplished and passionately in love. Jon was the one who wanted to be the astronaut. Laurel was the one who got accepted into the program. After she left for training, the Navy removed Jon from a powerful position in Florida and relocated him to Houston to a lesser position so that he could be a husband to an astronaut wife. It was something Laurel never asked for. She was a scientist, a mother, and Jon's partner, and she never liked the celebrity aspect of her job. Jon's move caused problems in the marriage. They struggled for a long time, but in the end made peace with themselves and grew as a couple before her mission. A great story, but a much better bet for a cable movie than a spec feature. Cable is a better market for female-driven projects because it has a big female audience. I despise saying this and furthering the Hollywood mentality, but very few female stars can open a movie. The box office numbers prove that, and it's a tough battle to fight unless you've got power behind you.

So in the case of Laurel Clark, since I own the rights to her story, the treatment is the best way to try to sell it. If we get passes on the project and I have nowhere else to take it, then I will have saved myself a year's worth of work writing the script.

Here's something to consider: if you can get your hands on the rights to a true story with merit, there are different ways you can negotiate the sale. You may not have the chance to write the script or adaptation, but you may possibly get a small credit that could further your career.

Treatments are useful with adaptations, if you're holding the rights to the book. We will cover this in Chapter 13.

11.

MOVIES FOR TELEVISION AND CABLE

IN ORDER FOR A SPEC script to be purchased, it must first be a good read. A good read is one in which you are compelled to turn the page. It's a story that immediately grabs you. The characters are alive. The dialogue is lean and has its own unique voice. Every line serves a purpose; every scene progresses the action forward and gives greater depth to the character. The narrative and locales instill pictures in your mind. There is powerful plot progression; there are powerful turning points and a strong beginning, middle, and end.

Each year, when it's voting time for the Academy and the Writers Guild of America for best screenplay, members are sent out scripts. What a great learning experience this is. This year I received *Michael Clayton*, *Juno*, *There Will Be Blood*, and *Lars and the Real Girl*, to name just a few.

I loved these scripts. With each read I was transported, and hours passed before I realized I hadn't refilled my coffee cup.

Creating scripts with this kind of direction and focus is a monumental battle for the novice, as well as the veteran writer. I have critiqued many speculation scripts written in the hopes of an eventual sale. Too often, these scripts wander off track. It is as though somewhere the writers have forgotten what they were writing about. Other times, I find myself excited by the material, only to discover that the script shifts gears and topples into that no-writers land called the "mess in the middle."

The script, unlike a horse, can't afford to lose momentum in hopes of a last push for the finish line. It must remain consistent throughout. How does the writer give the script this needed direction and focus? Where does a good screenplay begin? It begins with structure, the single most essential element of all screenplays. Attempting to write without thoroughly understanding structure is like driving blindly around looking for a house when you could ask for directions. Structure keeps the screenplay on track. It is the foundation on which everything is built.

THE TWO-HOUR MOVIE: THE BASIC THREE-ACT STRUCTURE

Movies for cable and television, as well as feature films, run approximately 95 to 105 pages. These acts are invisible; they are not spelled out in the script; they are for the purpose of structuring only. This page count is only approximate. Script length can vary according to story requirements. Cable movies can run on the short end of 95 pages, and features can run on the long end of 105 pages, but the days of turning in 120-page scripts are over. Screenplays are getting leaner and leaner. No executive or script reader today wants to take home a read that is over 110 pages. A script that runs long is dangerous, especially coming from a spec writer.

Act 1 is the setup. The setup, just as with the half-hour and one-hour scripts, establishes everything we need to know to get the story going:

The Setup (approximately 25 pages)
- Establishes the tone, the texture, and the place of the movie.
- Establishes the main characters and the circumstances of the story.
- Presents hook/inciting incident (by page 10).
- Establishes problem for the character/characters and dramatic need.
- Builds to the act 1 turning point (by page 25).

At the end of this 25-page unit of action, a turning point is introduced into the story that totally shifts the action around.

Act 2 is the confrontation. Here the character meets the majority of his or her obstacles. The act builds to another turning point that catapults the action and raises the stakes.

The Confrontation (approximately 50 pages)
- Presents obstacles to the character's dramatic need.
- Shows overriding, more-immediate needs taking over.
- Resolves issues, which then lead to greater complications.
- Creates rising conflict and the action.

- Raises the stakes for the character.
- Brings character to a crisis point (by page 75).

Act 3 builds to the climax and resolution of the story.

The Resolution (approximately 25 pages)

- Presents a moment of discovery and change for the character (emotional arc).
- Builds toward the climax.
- Has character achieve or not achieve his or her dramatic need.
- Resolves the story.

THREE-ACT STRUCTURE

ACT 1	ACT 2	ACT 3
Setup the characters; identify the hook; establish dramatic need (about 25 pages)	Obstacles to dramatic need; problem or problems resolved which leads to bigger complications (about 50 pages)	Resolution of problem or dramatic need achieved or failed (about 25 pages)

<<<<< CONFRONTATIONS >>>>>

conflict

conflict

rising action

hook   turning point   turning point

(*Note:* The vertical lines are imaginary divisions and only serve the purpose for the writer. These acts are not delineated on the script page.)

Figure 1.

At this point you may want to reread Chapter 2. The tools of teleplay writing absolutely apply to the cable and feature film. In episodic television, we are somewhat limited in our use of locales and narrative. But now, with the two-hour movie, we have free rein and can use these tools to their full potential. We are no longer limited by preset locations and formats or existing characters. It is now all ours to create: our imaginations, our craft . . . and our blank page.

By now, you should be looking at scripts differently. Reading in script format should be more comfortable to you. And you will note the same commonly used camera techniques turning up again and again. Various elements and components of scene construction should now be familiar. Ask yourself:

- Does each scene or sequence give us new and relevant information?
- Do we care about the characters?
- Does the writer use exposition successfully?
- What visuals are incorporated?
- What is the length of a scene or sequence? Where does one end and another begin?
- Is there pacing and flow?

Structure on the Page: Some Excerpts

To help us better understand structure, let's walk through various excerpts from a spec script I recently completed. *Who's Your Daddy* is the story of *two* single dads, mortal childhood

enemies, who show up in each other's lives after they discover
they're raising each other's ten-year-old-boys.

Unit 1 establishes the tone of the movie and the protagonist's (Joe's) "world." It was also important to establish the men
as childhood enemies, but this was backstory (their history), so
it had to be quick. The screenplay opens on a sequence of four
short scenes, then cuts to Joe as an adult. Notice the slug lines
here. They are used to indicate quick cuts every time the boy is
at bat.

WHO'S YOUR DADDY

FADE IN:

INT./EXT. KLING STREET ELEMENTARY SCHOOL — CREDITS OVER

Ten-year-old boys are standing in a circle playing
dodgeball. JOE CONNELLY, in the center, is an
impossible target. Definite future jock material.
Finally he is tagged.

HARVEY NEWMAN is the next up. He wears glasses and has
a runny nose and braces. Definite future nerd material.
Forget future, it doesn't get any worse. Harvey takes
the center of the circle and waits to get tagged—he is
always hit with the first ball. This time is no
exception. The boys razz him.

                    JOE
          Newman, you're such a loser!

INT. CLASSROOM — DAY

Harvey, seated behind Joe, takes out a small jar hidden in
his desk, removes a spider, and puts it down Joe's back.

Joe starts scratching. He looks down and spots the spider crawling out of his collar. He yells and jumps out of his seat. Harvey cracks up.

> HARVEY
>> Look at the big dude now!
>> Joe would like to squash the little
>> turd.

EXT. PIEDMONT MIDDLE SCHOOL — DAY

Fourteen-year-old Joe hooks a rope to Harvey's belt loop. Joe's buddies stand with him.

> JOE
>> Say it, Newman. Say it!

Joe pulls Harvey up a flagpole. His friends laugh.

> HARVEY
>> Okay, okay! I put your jock strap in
>> Mrs. McKenny's purse.

> JOE
>> You're such a jerk!

They leave him hanging there.

> HARVEY
>> Come back!
>> *Help somebody!*
>>> (screaming)
>> Get me out of here! Call the
>> principal. Get me down! I have no
>> feeling in my legs!

EXT. WEST SEATTLE HIGH SCHOOL — FOOTBALL FIELD — DAY

Harvey plays the tuba in the West Seattle Marching Band. He proudly marches in formation in his gold-buttoned jacket and high-tasseled hat.
The VARSITY TEAM runs out onto the field. Cheerleaders throw pom-poms. Joe snaps on his helmet and takes the line of scrimmage. He calls the signal.

SCOREBOARD. The fourth quarter. The game is tied, with the clock ticking down. Joe gets the ball, fakes a pass, plows through and scores the winning touchdown. The stadium goes wild. Teammates hoist Joe on their shoulders.

LATER

Cheerleaders hang on Joe. As Harvey passes, he turns the tuba toward Joe's ear and blows hard.

SUPER ON SCREEN: TWENTY YEARS LATER

EXT. LITTLE LEAGUE FIELD — DAY

J.J., a ten-year-old southpaw, is up at bat. He doesn't take the pitch. The UMP yells, *"Strike!"*
Joe, now in his midthirties and gone a bit paunchy, is seated with other parents in the stands.

> JOE
> Come on, it was low and on the
> outside, Ump!
> > (yelling to batter)
> You can do it, J.J. Just keep your
> eyes on the ball!

Another pitch. J.J takes a swing and misses.

> JOE
> Don't let it throw you, buddy.

J.J. takes another swing and strikes out.

THE NEXT TIME AT BAT

J.J. strikes out again. Joe speaks to the dad next to him.

> JOE
> That pitcher looks too big for Little
> League.

AND THE NEXT TIME AT BAT

> JOE
>> In center field, J.J.! Right over the
>> fence!

The pitcher winds up. J.J. wants this for his dad. He
swings with all his might. Strikes out again.

> JOE
>> Next time up!
>>> (to his neighbor)
>> I'm checking that kid out.

INT./EXT. MOVING IN JOE'S RX
CONVERTIBLE — DAY

> JOE
>> You win some, you lose some.

> J.J.
>> Man, I lose a lot.

> JOE
>> You're a jock, J.J., remember that.
>> Just like your old man. You've just
>> got to know it up here.

He removes his baseball cap and affectionately rubs his
head. J.J. takes out a BlackBerry and starts playing a
math game.

> JOE
>> How about a couple of dogs at McFly's?

> J.J.
>> They're bad for your cholesterol.

> JOE
>> We'll go to the Sports Pub with the
>> salad bar. The Kings are playing. What
>> do you say?

> J.J.
>> Yeah, I guess.

```
And we know J.J.'s heart isn't in it.

                    JOE
          Who loves you?

                    J.J.
          My old man, that's who.


FARTHER DOWN THE ROAD

They hit a red light. Joe looks over. The driver in the
next lane is a total knockout. She smiles at him.

                    JOE
          J.J., the left lane, check her out.

J.J. doesn't look up.

                    J.J.
          Yeah, I know. You're going to marry
          her and make her my mother.

                    JOE
          No, really, she's got it bad. She
          can't take her eyes off me.

The driver sits up higher and sticks out her chest.

                    JOE
          Oh, man, she just mouthed, "I want
          you."

Horns honk. J.J. doesn't look up.

                    J.J.
          Dad, the light changed.
```

What have we learned in the above scenes? J.J. obviously does not have his father's athletic ability. Joe is single, and a player. J.J. doesn't look up at the girl; he's more interested in playing math games on his BlackBerry. He agrees to the sports bar, to please his dad, and watches over his dad's diet. Father and son are very different.

· Later when they return home we even discover the boy keeps a chart on his dad's med's.

```
INT. MASTER BEDROOM — DAY

J.J. comes in and sets the pill on the dresser.

                    J.J.
          Your pill's on the dresser.

Joe comes out of the closet.

                    JOE
          You like the polo or the turtleneck?

                    J.J.
          Who are you going out with?

                    JOE
          Brooke.

                    J.J.
          Wear the polo. She got it for your
          birthday.

                    JOE
          I thought that was Jennifer.

                    J.J.
          She got you the Fear of
          Commitment. . . . Casey's late. She
          was supposed to be here at 7:00.

                    JOE
          Holy shit!

                    J.J.
          Dad! Mr. McGrath is going to kill me!
          I need our blood types for my science
          project tomorrow!
```

```
                          JOE
          I'll take care of it. It's covered,
          J.J. I've got the ball on it.
```

In the next scene DR. CASEY LEIB arrives. She's a secondary character and provides the romantic subplot. She's come to Joe's rescue many times. She draws blood from Joe and J.J. for J.J.'s class experiment.

As covered in Chapter 9, there are three areas in which we can reveal characters in film: through their *personal, professional,* and *private moments.* We next see Joe at his workplace and establish he is a sales rep for high-end sports outfitters. He gets an interrupting phone call on page 7. It's from Casey. She needs to talk to him in person. It might be best over a drink.

```
EXT. RESTAURANT — ON THE WATERFRONT — DAY

Sitting at a table in a busy restaurant, Casey nervously
consults her watch.

Joe enters the restaurant and walks over.

                          JOE
              So, what couldn't wait?

Joe sits down, takes her by the hands and looks deep
into her eyes.

                          JOE
              You've come to your senses and realize
              you want me. It's okay, Casey, we've
              been heading to this place for a long
              time.

She hesitates. What she is about to say is very
difficult.
```

                    CASEY
          J.J.'s got a very rare blood type, and
          given yours and Linda's, the chances
          are very slim he could be your son.

                    JOE
          Huh?

                    CASEY
          J.J. is not your natural son.

He takes a beat.

                    JOE
           . . . You're screwing with my head,
          right?

                    CASEY
          I did the DNA test.

                    JOE
          So you messed up.

                    CASEY
          You're questioning me as a doctor?

                    JOE
          Son-of-a-bitch!

                    CASEY
          Joe, he will always be your son. The
          tests just say he's not your natural
          son.

                    JOE
          That's impossible. Run the tests
          again!

                    CASEY
          I ran them twice . . . I delivered
          him. I feel awful, Joe.

                    JOE
          I'm really sorry for you, Casey! He's
          mine! I raised him alone. I changed
          his diapers. When he had the croup, I
          sat with him under the blankets.
                    (MORE)

                JOE (CONT'D)
I was the fairy godmother who put
five bucks under his pillow every
time he lost a tooth. I threw him his
first ball!

He takes a moment. This is inconceivable.

                JOE
How the hell could something like this
happen?

                CASEY
It was crazy that night. Women were
lined up in the halls, and babies
were everywhere. Don't you remember?
It was nine months after the
blackout.

                JOE
It's all very blurry. I was getting
married. Linda's father was pointing a
gun at my nuts.

                CASEY
According to the records, six girls
and two boys were born on my shift.
The boys were born minutes apart.

Joe buries his head in his hands. He hates to ask—

                JOE
. . . Who's the other boy?

                CASEY
He was born to an Emily Newman. His
parents still live here in Seattle.
His name is Hector.

                JOE
HECTOR? . . . They named him
Hector? . . . Jesus, that's what you
call a bloodhound.

A waitress comes up.

                WAITRESS
What can I get for you?

```
                    JOE
          A bottle of Scotch.
                    (then, to Casey)
          What are you drinking?
```

The *hook* happens on page 10—it's the early action that grabs
an audience, or sells a pitch. Think of it as a moment that would
run on the trailers, or somewhere on a tagline. It's the moment
when Joe discovers J.J. is not his boy.

In *unit 2*, Joe has learned the truth. Now what will he do
about it? He must take some action. Notice how conflict in every
scene forces the character's next move.

```
EXT. NEWMAN HOME — EARLY EVENING

A Prius pulls into a driveway.


ACROSS THE STREET


INT. JOE'S RX — SAME

The top is up. Joe ZOOMS IN WITH BINOCULARS. He spots a
man and a boy getting out of the car, but he can only
see them from the back. They disappear inside.
Nothing through the curtains. He SCANS THE YARD.
Flowers are planted in perfect symmetry along the
walkway. On the side of the house is a vegetable garden.
He ZOOMS IN TIGHT. All the plants and herbs are tagged.
One small section reads "Pesto garden."

                    JOE
          Who plants a pesto garden?


EXT. NEWMAN HOUSE — CONTINUOUS

Joe walks to the door. He can hear voices inside.
```

                         HARVEY (O.S.)
              You have two D's!

                         HECTOR (O.S.)
              Yeah, but I've got spirit and
              enthusiasm. And I'm good with computers.

                         HARVEY (O.S.)
              That's an after-school activity.

                         HECTOR (O.S.)
              It counts for something. Look what
              happened to Bill Gates.

A tuba starts playing the scales. Whoever's blowing is
off-key. Joe rings the bell and nervously waits. After
a moment the door opens. It's HECTOR, with a tuba
around his neck.
Joe, at first, is speechless. The boy has his exact
coloring.

                         JOE
                 . . . Hi.

                         HECTOR
              Hi.

                         JOE
              Are your parents home?

                         HECTOR
                         (yelling)
              Hey, Dad, there's a stranger at the
              door. I didn't look through the
              peephole like I was supposed to.

                         HARVEY (O.S.)
              Hector!

                         HECTOR
              Sorry.

Hector leaves and HARVEY appears. He is now in his
midthirties, his glasses and braces are gone, and he's
quite attractive. Joe doesn't recognize him.

                         JOE
              Ah . . . Mr. Newman?

> HARVEY
> What do you want?

Hector starts playing the tuba in the b.g.

> JOE
> We have a situation . . . Is your wife
> home? Because we should talk where no
> one can hear us.

As Harvey steps outside onto the porch, a RINGER goes off.

> HARVEY
> Make it quick. In a minute and forty-
> five seconds my noodles will go limp.

> JOE
> Ten years ago you walked out of the
> hospital with the wrong kid.

> HARVEY
> Excuse me?

> JOE
> I'm not pointing any fingers. We all
> make mistakes. I did the same thing.

> HARVEY
> What?

> JOE
> We had boys born minutes apart at the
> same hospital. Maybe somebody worked
> too many shifts, or some fruitcake
> broke out of the psych ward, and
> played "Name That Baby!" The point is,
> there was a major screw-up and we went
> home with the wrong kids. It didn't
> turn out wrong. I love my boy, and I'm
> sure you love yours, but those are the
> facts.

> HARVEY
> The only fruitcake around here is you.
> I'm not surprised. It happens with
> aging jocks. You've been hit by too
> many pigskins and hockey pucks.

Joe looks at Harvey closer. Something about this guy is
making him feel very uncomfortable.

                    JOE
            . . . You're starting to look
            familiar. Do you know me?

                    HARVEY
            Unfortunately, yes.

The tuba plays one long off-key note. It sounds like a
long fart. It dawns on Joe.

                    JOE
            Wait a minute . . . did you go to
            Kling Elementary and Piedmont Middle
            School? . . . Yeah, you're the nerd
            with the braces and glasses who put the
            spider down my back . . . Newman . . .
            Harvey Newman! We went to West Seattle
            High together. You were in the band.
            You put my jock strap in Mrs. McKenny's
            purse. How come you never left me

                    JOE (CONT'D)
            alone? You were always in my face! You
            made my life miserable!

                    HARVEY
            I hated you. You tormented me and
            called me names. You pulled me up
            the flagpole and left me hanging for
            so long I almost lost the use of my
            legs. I hated myself because of you.
            You took the little self-esteem I
            had and mashed it into the ground. I
            spent five years in therapy because
            of you!

Harvey has worked himself into a frenzy. Joe steps back.

                    JOE
            Maybe you should have stayed in there
            longer. You're still a whack job.
                    (a horrible thought)

                    JOE (CONT'D)
        I was done with you . . . Now you're
        back like Freddy Krueger.
                    (another thought)
        Of all the fathers in the world, my
        kid got you.

                    HARVEY
        He's *my* kid, and his name is Hector.

                    JOE
        Don't you know the impact names have
        on kids!

                    HARVEY
        Hector was a great warrior in ancient
        Troy.

                    JOE
        Today, in Seattle, he's a total loser.
        And that thing he blows that looks
        like Jabba the Hutt . . .

                    HARVEY
        It is called a tuba!

                    JOE
        It figures you couldn't steer him
        toward something smaller, like the
        saxophone. Chicks dig the sax. What
        about his self-esteem? Maybe I should
        have a little say in this.

We hear Harvey's TIMER GOES OFF.

                    HARVEY
        You're delusional. If you're not off
        my property in one minute I'm calling
        the police.

                    JOE
        Call Dr. Leib at Valley Hospital.
        She'll show you the tests. She can
        back up everything I've told you.

Harvey slams the door in Joe's face.

INT. HARVEY'S HOUSE — FOLLOWING

Harvey and Hector sit at the table with cloth napkins.

> HECTOR
> Who was that guy?

> HARVEY
> We went to school together a long time
> ago. He was trying to sell me
> something.

> HECTOR
> He looked at me weird.

Fresh broccoli is placed on the table, along with every
color of vegetable, whole wheat noodles, and milk.
Hector reacts.

> HECTOR
> I need to eat a corn dog once in a
> while like normal kids.

> HARVEY
> This is a perfectly balanced meal.
> It's what I do.

> HECTOR
> For old people. You're a geriatric
> nutritionist. I'm ten! What if this
> stuff isn't good for me? I could grow
> up needing a hip replacement.

> HARVEY
> Hector, that's ridiculous. Eat.

They eat in silence a moment. Harvey studies Hector,
bothered by something.

> HARVEY
> Tell me what you think about the tuba.

> HECTOR
> (by rote)
> In marching band it serves as the
> entire bass for the brass section.

```
                    HARVEY
         No, I mean how do you feel about
         playing it?

                    HECTOR
         I do it because I love you. As father
         and son, I think we need more give and
         take in our relationship.

                    HARVEY
         You're doing your homework!
```

The scenes above provide new and pertinent information (exposition). Harvey and Hector are very different. Joe hears Hector off screen (O.S.), trying to soft-pedal his dad. From the sound of the tuba in the b.g. (background) the boy is obviously not a musician.

The scene between Joe and Harvey establishes the negative impact they've had on each other. In the dinner scene we learn what Harvey does for a living and that Hector is a bit of a con, like Joe. In a screenplay all dialogue must serve a purpose and process the plot forward. Everything nonfunctional must go.

The next scene takes place on the golf course where Casey tells Joe that Harvey came to the hospital to see her. He was very upset. She found him very nice and kind of cute. According to him they have had quite a history. "Spooky," says Joe. "Creepier than the movie *The Ring*." The *button* is we hear a phone ringing (O.S.) and cut to the next scene.

```
INT. JOE'S HOUSE — BEDROOM — NIGHT

WE HOLD TIGHT ON A PHONE. It continues to RING. The clock
reads 1:00 a.m. Joe reaches over and grabs the phone.
```

> HARVEY (O.S.)
> Meet me in the park tomorrow.

> JOE
> Who is this?

> HARVEY (O.S.)
> In neutral territory. The bench on the
> east side of Paddlewheel Park. Three
> p.m. Bring no one with you.

He hangs up, leaving Joe staring at the receiver.

EXT. PADDLEWHEEL PARK — 3:00 PM — THE FOLLOWING DAY

Joe sits on the bench waiting. A clock strikes three. A
man in an overcoat, hat, and sunglasses approaches. It's
very obvious it's Harvey with a newspaper under his arm.
He sits down.

> HARVEY
> Don't look at me. Stare forward.

> JOE
> You're kidding, right? You're still a
> psycho.

> HARVEY
> In spite of what the tests say, Hector
> is still my son.

> JOE
> I feel the same way about J.J.

> HARVEY
> J.J.?

> JOE
> Joe Junior. I named him after his old
> man.

> HARVEY
> This is an impossible situation.

> JOE
> Maybe we should sue somebody.

                    HARVEY
Who, the fruitcake that broke out of
the psych ward and played "Name That
Baby"?

                    JOE
We don't know for sure if that's what
happened.

                    HARVEY
Of course we don't!

                    JOE
But we don't know for sure that it
didn't.

                    HARVEY
Don't you ever stop!

                    JOE
All I'm saying is, somebody should be
held accountable. It's gross
negligence.

                    HARVEY
So let's all go on "Larry King" and
talk about it!

                    JOE
You're wound up tight. Maybe you
should try exercise.

                    HARVEY
 . . . Look, what if we don't do
anything?

                    JOE
You mean we act like this never
happened?

                    HARVEY
Hector lost his mother five years ago.
He's already been through a lot.

                    JOE
 . . . I'm sorry.

                    HARVEY
How do you think your wife would feel
about it?

                    JOE
We were never really married.

                    HARVEY
J.J.'s a bastard?

                    JOE
We tied the knot in the
hospital . . . under duress. Linda's
old man had a German Luger.

                    HARVEY
  . . . A shotgun wedding.

                    JOE
Man, he was scary. I think he served
in the Luftwaffe. The next day we
got it annulled. She didn't want the
responsibility and left.

                    HARVEY
That poor child . . .
you've been his only role model?
                    (stopping himself)

              HARVEY (CONT'D)
No, I can't go there. It's not good
for either boy. What matters is the
love and time we've given them, not
our DNA.

                    JOE
Yeah, Angelina Jolie says there's no
difference between adopting a kid and
having one. You love them both the
same.
                    (off Harvey's look)
Anything that woman says, I back her a
hundred percent.

                    HARVEY
It's better we go our separate ways.

                    JOE
Yeah, it's the only solution.

```
                    HARVEY
          I don't get involved in your
          life . . .

                    JOE
          And you stay out of my face.

                    HARVEY
          No more contact.
                    (a beat, then)
          Can I see a picture of J.J.? It's only
          fair. You saw Hector.

Joe shows him a picture. Harvey's moved.

                    JOE
          He's a great kid, and smart. He always
          makes the honor roll . . . Tell me
          something about Hector.

                    HARVEY
          He's got great spirit and enthusiasm.
          He could make a fortune in sales.

                    JOE
                    (smiles)
          That's what I do.

Harvey takes a deep breath.

                    HARVEY
          I absolutely have no say in how you
          raise my son.

                    JOE
          And how you raise my son is none of my
          business.
```

The men have made a pact. In *unit 3*, they are unable to keep it.

They both peek into "their" boys' lives. Joe hires a detective and learns Hector's schedule. Wearing a disguise he watches him in horticulture club and discovers he loves tulips. For fun,

Hector hangs out with seniors at his father's rest home and flirts with an old woman.

Harvey, disguised as a crossing guard, overhears J.J. giving bookmaking odds to a friend. He tails Joe and J.J. to a Blockbuster and is aghast at what they leave in the drop box. He sees Joe's girl-friend leave after spending the night while J.J. is in the house.

Below is a sequence of scenes leading to the act 1 turning point (the courtroom). Notice where the scenes start and end and how they build.

```
EXT. HARVEY'S HOUSE — HALLOWEEN — NIGHT

Harvey and Hector are both dressed as Sponge Bob. They
can hardly make it out the front door.

                    HECTOR
          I don't like this costume. I think
          it's stupid.

                    HARVEY
          Sponge Bob is very popular.

                    HECTOR
          But what if it rains?


INT. JOE'S HOUSE — LIVING ROOM — SAME TIME

J.J. is standing in a tux with a girl his age in high
heels, makeup, and a strapless dress.
A flash goes off. Joe's current girlfriend, Brooke, is
taking the picture.

                    J.J.
          I liked that Homer Simpson costume,
          and that Sponge Bob was really funny.

                    JOE
          J.J., this is way cooler. All guys
          want to be Bond; he gets all the
          babes.
```

> BROOKE
> You both look hot.

EXT./INT. DRIVING IN THE PRIUS — JOE'S NEIGHBORHOOD

They pull through the gate of Joe's neighborhood.

> HECTOR (O.S.)
> How come we can't trick or treat where
> we always do?

> HARVEY (O.S.)
> We'll get better candy here.

> HECTOR (O.S.)
> You don't let me eat it anyway, so
> what's the point?

EXT. A NEIGHBORHOOD STREET — NIGHT

Harvey and Hector are following a group of kids. We see
J.J. and the girl with them up ahead.

> HARVEY
> Hurry up, we're falling behind.

They hurry to the porch, bumping into everything.
The door opens, and everybody yells "Trick or treat!"
J.J., who is standing in front, pulls out a gun and
points it at the lady passing out Godiva bars.

> J.J.
> The name is Bond, James Bond.

> LADY
> And who's the pretty lady on your arm?

> J.J.
> She's Pussy Galore.

> HARVEY
> (yelling)
> Okay! *That's it!*

Harvey turns, knocking into Little Bo Peep. Her treat
bag falls on top of a pumpkin and catches on fire. Harvey
screams at the top of his lungs.

> HARVEY
> *Fire!*

He grabs her bag and runs with it into the yard.

> HARVEY
> *Fire!* Everybody out of the way. Stay clear!

Joe and Brooke run over. Everybody's watching.

Harvey drops the bag and leaps on top of it. His sponge bounces, and he rolls over into a somersault. The fire's extinguished, but Tootsie Rolls and Big Hunks are stuck all over him.

> HECTOR
> (to the kids)
> We're not related; we just have the same costume.

> HARVEY
> (to Joe)
> I've had it! I can't do this anymore.

> JOE
> Hey, you broke your word!

> HARVEY
> I saw you at the rest home!

> J.J.
> (to Hector re: Harvey)
> Who's he?

> HECTOR
> Sponge Bob.

> HARVEY
> Stay out of this, Bond! And your

> HARVEY (CONT'D)
> friend Pussy here should go home to her mother!

INT. COURTROOM — DAY

Joe and Harvey stand before a Judge Judy—like judge.

JUDGE
(to Harvey)
Let me get this straight. You don't
like the way he's raising your son.

HARVEY
Correct.

JUDGE
And you don't like the way he's
raising yours.

JOE
That's right.

JUDGE
(re: paperwork)
The sons you're raising aren't yours.

HARVEY
They're ours, but—

JUDGE
Shut up! It says right here your sons
were switched at birth, so you're
raising the wrong kids. Correct?

JOE
We don't feel that way.

JUDGE
I don't care how you feel. Have you
told them the truth?

HARVEY
It would be too traumatic.

JUDGE
From what I'm looking at, it would be
terrifying.

HARVEY
Your Honor, he's an unfit father. He's
raising a delinquent and a womanizer.
My son is involved in some kind of
bookmaking operation! He is ten years
old and has a girlfriend named Pussy!

JOE

He's the one who's unfit. This man is
damaging my boy. The only thing he
likes are tulips and old people.

JUDY

Which boy are we talking about, the
bookie or the tuba player?

JOE   HARVEY

The tuba player.   The bookie.

JOE

I'm raising his kid, the bookie, to be
a healthy normal boy. He's
raising my kid, the tuba player, to
grow up repressed, and end up in some
airport men's room tapping his feet!

HARVEY

He lets women sleep over!
          (to Joe)
I saw that woman leave your house!
Do you know how damaging that is?
No, because you think Dr. Laura is a
cleaning fluid! And I saw what you
dropped off at Blockbuster, a movie
called *Snatch*! Can you believe that,
Your Honor, it's disgusting!

JOE

It's about a jewel heist, you idiot!

JUDGE

          (pounding the gavel)
Get over it! You should both be
ashamed of yourselves!

They shut up.

JUDGE

According to the affidavits your
attorneys filed, you agreed to keep
your living arrangements the way they
are.

                    HARVEY
          Yes, but we feel it's in our
          children's best interest to have some
          kind of visitation . . .

                    JOE
          Like a day every other week, or we
          could alternate the days . . .

                    JUDGE
          This is not "Deal or No Deal!" Do I
          look like Howie Mandel?

                    JOE/HARVEY
          No, Your Honor.

                    JUDGE
          The court will allow you one weekend a
          month with one condition—you tell your
          boys the truth.

EXT. COURTHOUSE STEPS — DAY

Differences aside, they have to consider the boys.

                    JOE
          How do we do this?

                    HARVEY
          We can't just spring it on them. They
          have to get to know each other first.

Act 2, the confrontation.

Now Joe and Harvey must work together. Differences aside, their goal is to make it as easy as they possibly can on the boys. The confrontation runs approximately 45 to 55 pages. Again I break it down into three units, each running about 15 to 18 pages. As we discussed in Chapters 7 and 8, each unit must accomplish something to move the story forward.

In *unit 1,* all attempts for Joe and Harvey to befriend their boys fail. At the rest home, where J.J. thinks they're meeting an old friend of his dad's, Harvey's running late. Joe tries to occupy himself. Notice how conflict plays out in every scene.

EXT. REST HOME — GROUNDS — DAY

Joe's got a group of seniors on the lawn. He speaks to
WILLIAM, on a walker.

> JOE
> Okay, Willie here's the goalie.

> WILLIAM
> I have trouble standing.

> JOE
> That's no problem. Just lean on your
> walker. We're going to use it for the
> goal post.

Joe takes a T-shirt and ties it to the walker.

> JOE
> What you're all going to do is use
> your croquet mallets to get the ball
> through Willie's walker. Everybody in
> wheelchairs—you're the defensive line.
> You'll get handicaps so it's fair
> play. Remember, people, it's not age,
> it's attitude. You're all looking a
> little dead around here.

J.J. whispers into his dad's ear.

> J.J.
> They almost are Dad.

> JOE
> Look alive, everybody! Give it all
> you've got.

> J.J.
> I don't think this is a good idea.

DISSOLVE TO:

LATER

Harvey and Hector exit the building. They hear yelling
coming from the grounds.
A game is in play, with Joe coaching. ADDIE swings her
mallet, the ball heads for the goal posts. A senior, MR.
HANLAN, intercepts. Harvey reacts.

                    HARVEY
          Oh, my God!

                    JOE
          Go! Go! Go! Who's blocking . . .
          where's the defense?

The wheelchairs aggressively move in.

                    JOE
          . . . Ten yards . . . she's going to
          sink it. Watch it! Everybody keep your
          eyes on the ball!

Mr. Hanlan tries to block MILTON, in a wheelchair,
and is thrown in the air. Milton collides head-on
into another wheelchair. They both topple over. Harvey
screams.

                    HARVEY
          Nooooooooo!

INT. SUNRISE NURSING STATION — HALLWAY — DAY

Harvey, Joe, and the boys wait outside the door.

                    HARVEY
          Our plans with the boys are totally
          ruined! There will be no dinner
          because I will be spending the night
          filling out accident reports! Your
          stupidity has placed this institution
          and the people we care for at grave
          risk. If I lose my job over this, I'm
          suing you for personal damages.

A NURSE comes out.

                    NURSE
          They want to see the coach.

                    HARVEY
          There's no time for that. We need to
          fill out reports.

                MR. HANLAN (O.S.)
          To hell with paperwork! We want the
          coach!

Harvey, who is totally frustrated, opens the door and
follows Joe inside. The boys now are left alone.

                    J.J.
          I'm J.J.

                    HECTOR
          I'm Hector.

                    J.J.
          Your dad was Sponge Bob.

                    HECTOR
          I know. Yours came to our door trying
          to sell us something.

INT. NURSE'S STATION

Mr. Hanlan sits in a neck brace, and Milton sits with
his leg wrapped in bandages.

                    MR. HANLAN
             So, Coach, what's the name of this
             game we were playing?

Joe tries to think up something.

                    JOE
             . . . Ah, it's soccer for seniors;
             they call it . . . suture ball.

                    MR. HANLAN
             It gets the old blood going, huh,
             Milton?

```
                    MILTON
          That last play was a killer.

                    JOE
          Yeah, that's a tricky maneuver.

                    WILLIE
          What's it called?


Harvey rolls his eyes.

                    JOE
            . . . The Double Fogie.
```

They take the boys bowling and fight over who has the superior balls. Harvey accidentally drops his on Joe's foot and it lands him in the emergency room.

On Thanksgiving, Harvey, a gourmet cook, makes a turkey. They argue over Quentin Tarantino, R ratings, and why Joe won't allow the movie *Bambi* in the house: it's physiologically damaging to children. Joe presses the oven's self-lock cleaning button and after having to disassemble the door, they sit down to a burnt turkey.

This whole fiasco's been too weird and the boys know something's up. After dinner, they sit on the sofa with Joe and Harvey facing them.

```
                    JOE
          So, boys, here's the deal.

                    HECTOR
          Oh man, here it comes.

                    HARVEY
          We found out something a few weeks ago
          that, well, changed our lives and it
          will change yours too.

                    J.J.
          I don't want my life to change.
```

                         HECTOR
Neither do I.

                          JOE
I felt the same way, but it has
changed, and you need to know about it.

                         J.J.
Is it good news or bad news?

                        HECTOR
It sucks. Just look at their faces.

                        HARVEY
Hector, we don't use that word—

                          JOE
This isn't the time to worry about
words.

                        HECTOR
Then it's really going to suck. That's
why they filled us with tryptophan.

                         J.J.
What's that?

                        HECTOR
It's in the turkey. It's this amino
acid that deadens your senses and
numbs you. You get drowsy, and then
it knocks you out. The only thing you
remember is waking up.

                        HARVEY
Hector, that's enough.

Hector shuts up. Nobody talks. Joe picks up the slack.

                          JOE
   . . . When babies are born, they're
ID'd and tagged, and then they're
rolled into a room where they're
viewed.

                        HARVEY
By their parents, not by medical
examiners. It isn't an autopsy!
                        (MORE)

                         HARVEY(CONT'D)
                          (to the boys)
          They're all cozy and warm in bassinets.
          They wear ID bracelets on their wrists,
          not tags on their toes, and they're
          wrapped up like little burritos.

                         J.J.
          Will somebody tell us what's going on!

                         HARVEY
           . . . You were born in the same
          hospital on the same day.

                         JOE
          What are the odds, huh?

                         HARVEY
          Somehow your wristbands got switched,
          and we went home with each other's
          babies.

The boys sit dumbstruck for a long moment. Hector looks
at Joe.

                         HECTOR
          You're my dad?

                         J.J.
          He's not your dad. You don't even know
          him!
                          (to Harvey)
          And you're not my dad either!

                         HARVEY
          Joe raised you, so he'll always be
          your dad. But, like it or not, I'm
          your biological father.

                         J.J.
          You're a liar!

                         JOE
          J.J.!

                         J.J.
          You don't want me anymore!

                    JOE
Of course I want you. You'll always be
my boy.

                    HECTOR
              (to Harvey)
I hate you!

                    HARVEY
You don't mean that.

                    HECTOR
Yes, I do.

                    HARVEY
I love you, Hector. I will always love
you, and nothing is ever going to
change that.

                    JOE
In fact, nothing's going to change,
except for one weekend a month . . .

                    HECTOR
What happens then?

                    JOE
You'll stay with me, so I can get to
know you better . . .

                    HARVEY
And J.J., we'll do the same so that we
can get better acquainted.

                    J.J.
I don't want to know you better. I'm
not going.

                    HECTOR
Me either. It *sucks*, and I'm not doing it!

                    HARVEY
Stop saying that word.

                    HECTOR
Sucks . . .
sucks . . .
sucks . . .
sucks.

```
                         J.J.
                    (to Joe/Harvey)
          I hate you both.
                    (to Hector)
          And I hate you!

                       HECTOR
          I hate you too.


INT. HECTOR'S BEDROOM — SAME

Hector runs inside. J.J. follows him in.

                       HECTOR
          Stay out; you hate me.

                         J.J.
          I hate them more.


INT. HARVEY'S LIVING ROOM — SAME


                       HARVEY
          That went well.

                        JOE
          "Like it or not, I'm your biological
          father." That was raw.
```

A major problem for the men is resolved: the boys now know the truth, but they rebel.

Unit 2 provides more obstacles to the characters. The men have their first weekend with the boys. Using a SERIES OF SHOTS here is very helpful. It establishes time and place without having to use slugs and go into detail.

```
SERIES OF SHOTS — DAY

Harvey and J.J. go to a home-and-garden show. Harvey
watches a demonstration of a vegetable shredder. J.J.
```

stands behind him playing math games on his Blackberry.
Joe takes Hector to a ball game. His only interest is the
junk food. They don't talk; he just eats, and Joe eats along
with him—chili dogs, corn dogs, curly fries, and nachos.
Harvey takes J.J. for a ride in a paddleboat. J.J. tries
to cover his face so nobody will see him.

INT. JOE'S HOUSE — DAY

Joe's lying on the floor, sick from all the junk food.

> JOE
>
> I don't feel so good.

> HECTOR
>
> J.J. said you dated a Victoria's
> Secret model. I want to meet her.

> JOE
>
> She's gone.

> HECTOR
>
> What happened to her?

> JOE
>
> Leonardo DiCaprio.

> HECTOR
>
> So what are we going to do now? Let's
> fly to Vegas.

> JOE
>
> What?

> HECTOR
>
> They call it a family playground.
> We're a family, right?

> JOE
>
> You're out of your mind.

> HECTOR
>
> Why?

> JOE
>
> For starters, it's crossing state
> lines with a minor. I could get life
> in prison for kidnapping.

                    HECTOR
    But you're my dad.

                     JOE
    That's a gray area. Maybe I'd get
    fifteen to twenty.

                    HECTOR
    So who's going to know?

                     JOE
    Don't you ever stop!

                    HECTOR
    The way I see it, you owe me.

                     JOE
    Oh, really?

                    HECTOR
    There I was, screaming out to you, but
    I couldn't talk yet, I couldn't yell
    "Dad!" But you should have recognized
    me anyway.

                     JOE
    How?

                    HECTOR
    Because all beasts in the animal
    kingdom recognize their own.

                     JOE
    You're good.

                    HECTOR
    Think about what I've been through for
    the last ten years.

                     JOE
    You're really good. They won't let you
    in the casinos.

                    HECTOR
    Who cares? There's a Defcon convention
    going on right now.

                     JOE
    What's Defcon?

```
                     HECTOR
          Oh, man, only the coolest high-tech
          computer show in the whole world. And
          at the Stratosphere there's this ride
          called the X-Scream that shoots you
          three hundred sixty-five feet out over
          a rooftop. And there's all-you-can-eat
          buffets, and Southwest has flights that
          leave every hour. Please!
```

We now cut between Joe and Harvey and their progressively bad weekends.

J.J. insists Harvey dig up his spring crocuses because he planted them one centimeter off. His anal-retentive behavior is a little too close for comfort. Harvey discovers the boy has perfect pitch and gives him a tuba lesson. J.J. turns the tuba in his face and blows in his ear. While cooking, Harvey shows him how to finesse tossing salt. J.J. tries it and it lands in Harvey's eyes.

In Las Vegas, Hector forgets to bring Joe's meds. He encourages him to eat shellfish (which he's allergic to) and tells him all about the shocking goings-on at the rest home. Joe leaves Hector waiting in the long line at the X-Scream to place a bet at the sports book. Hector pays a kid to save his place, sneaks off to an all-girl review, hides under a table, and takes pictures of a showgirl in a thong with his Razr phone. When he's chased out, he leaves the phone behind.

Joe returns with a puffed-up face to an innocent-looking Hector standing back in line. The sequence ends on the X-Scream as they shoot over the observation deck and hang 900 feet in the air, Joe screaming his swollen head off.

Their weekends send both men to the doctor's office.

INT. CASEY'S OFFICE — DAY

Casey is checking Joe's tests.

> CASEY
> Your cholesterol has jumped off the
> charts.

> JOE
> Casey, had I walked out of the
> hospital with the right kid, I'd be
> dead right now. Thank God I'll only
> see him once a month. He's a very bad
> influence. He makes me do stupid shit.

> CASEY
> And this stupid shit you can't say no
> to?

> JOE
> He's wild like Linda. He gets the same
> crazed look in his eye. On the flight
> back he was eyeballing all the flight
> attendants. That's not normal for a
> ten-year-old. His mother was seriously
> oversexed. That's why I was attracted
> to her.

> CASEY
> So I guess your genes played no part
> in this?

> JOE
> My puberty was normal.

> CASEY
> Except for the fact you're still in it.

INT. DOCTOR'S OFFICE — DAY

The door opens, and Harvey jumps. The DOCTOR checks his
chart.

> DOCTOR
> Hello, Harvey. What are we seeing you
> for?

```
                    HARVEY
          I need some kind of medication. I just
          need it once a month.

                    DOCTOR
          You adamantly oppose drugs.

                    HARVEY
          Yes, I do . . . but I've discovered
          there's a time for every purpose . . .
```

Embarrassed by his choice of words, he finishes the lyric—

```
                    HARVEY
          . . . unto Heaven.

                    DOCTOR
                    (flatly)
          Turn . . .
          turn . . .
          turn.
                    (and then)
          What kind of drug do you think you
          need?

                    HARVEY
          Something that numbs me to outer
          stimuli . . . so I don't react to
          anal-retentive, obsessive-compulsive
          personalities. I want to be cognizant
          and conscious, but in a peaceful state
          so that nothing bothers me.

                    DOCTOR
          Heroin's illegal.
```

In *Unit 3,* the stakes rise, building the conflict leading to
plot point 2.

Joe returns home to find tulips on the table and the sound of a
tuba coming from J.J.'s bedroom. Hector calls: he lost his cell phone
and his dad wants it. He dialed the number and a lady in Las Vegas
answered named Lauren. She's a dancer in one of the shows. Joe

loses it. Harvey could call the number, he'll know where they were. He tells J.J. to pack his things; he's dropping him off at Casey's.

Notice the pacing and timing of the scenes. Rarely do the scenes exceed two pages (2 minutes). The device *intercut* allows us to go between two locales without having to use slugs.

                         JOE
                Cell phone . . .
                cell phone . . .

He finds Hector's number and dials. Somebody picks up.

                         JOE (cont'd)
                Hello? I'm the father of the boy
                who lost his Razr phone. He's been
                grounded and has lost all phone
                privileges . . .
                Yeah . . . tough love, but what are
                you going to do? *NO,* no need to mail
                it! I'll be in tonight to pick it up.
                Thank you so much.

He hangs up and hurriedly shoves J.J.'s schoolwork into his knapsack. He spots something. It's a DVD of *Bambi*. This is the final affront.

                         JOE
                Goddamn you, Harvey!

INT. STRATOSPHERE HOTEL — DINING ROOM — NIGHT

A maître d' seats Joe at a booth near the stage.

                         WAITER
                She's the one at the end of the line.
                Just look up.

ON STAGE

The lights. The fanfare. The curtains open and the line of showgirls strut on stage. Joe looks up and

spots Lauren. His mouth drops open. She is the most
beautiful of the bunch.

>   JOE
>   Oh, man . . .

She passes by in her thong.

>   JOE
>   Holy shit!

INT. BACKSTAGE — LATER

Lauren hands Joe the phone.

>   LAUREN
>   He sounds like a sweet kid.

>   JOE
>   Excuse me?

>   LAUREN
>   I don't know how it got backstage,
>   but I hope he doesn't get in too much
>   trouble.

>   JOE
>   Who?

>   LAUREN
>   Your son.

>   JOE
>   Oh, right. I really struggle with
>   where to draw the line. It's tough
>   being a single parent.

>   LAUREN
>   I know. I have three of my own.

Suddenly she's not so attractive.

>   JOE
>   Oh, is that so?

At the rest home the following morning a group of seniors,
all wearing athletic gear, confront Harvey. They took Coach

Joe's advice and have been working out. They're fit as fiddles and they're not playing shuffleboard! They want Coach Joe and they want to play suture ball! They threaten Harvey with a sit-in. Meanwhile at school, Hector makes a call from a pay phone.

```
EXT. PAYPHONE — DAY


                    HECTOR
          Was she hot?


INTERCUT:


INT. STRIKE SPORTS — JOE'S OFFICE — DAY

Joe is on the phone.

                    JOE
          Do you have any idea what I went
          through to get that phone?

                    HECTOR
          Was she the hottest one there?

                    JOE
          Yeah, unbelievable.

                    HECTOR
          Then she was at the end of the line.

                    JOE
          How do you know?

                    HECTOR
          Yes! What are the odds!

                    JOE
          . . . Wait a minute . . .
          oh God . . . I don't believe
          you . . . you got into the theater!

                    HECTOR
          You need to marry her.
```

                    JOE
        What?

                    HECTOR
        That way, every month when I come
        visit, I get to see her.

                    JOE
        I'd have to be crazy to marry a woman
        with three kids. You're more than
        enough! With J.J. that would make five
        of you. I'd rather be staked to an
        anthill! Something's not right with
        you. You need some form of therapy.
        You're ten years old! What happened to
        Transformers and Dinobots?

                    HECTOR
        Open the flip and hit "my pix." We
        need to erase the pictures before we
        give the phone back to Dad.

Joe freezes.

                    JOE
        What pictures?

                    HECTOR
        The ones of her in a thong!

                    JOE
                  (yelling)
        You took pictures of her in a thong!
        Oh, God! I'm screwed. I dropped it off
        last night on the way back from the
        airport!

INT. SUNRISE REST HOME — DAY

The seniors stage a sit-in in a rec room. Harvey holds
up Hector's Razr phone.

                    HARVEY
        I'm calling Coach Joe right now. I'm
        pressing the send button.

Instead, he hits "my pix"; a picture of Lauren in a
thong appears ON THE SCREEN. Harvey gasps. He throws
the phone in the air. It lands in Mr. Hanlan's lap. He
looks at it.

                    MR. HANLAN
          Buns of steel.

INT. SUNSET REST HOME — HARVEY'S OFFICE — DAY

The blinds open up, and Joe looks out. The seniors are
holding their sit-in.

                    HARVEY
          This is your fault!

                    JOE
          There's a tuba in my house and tulips
          on my table.

                    HARVEY
          There was never a problem in this
          place until you showed up.

                    JOE
          What did you do to my kid? He's in my
          face playing bad-ass jokes. You handed
          me back some kind of mutant
          cross-over!

                    HARVEY
          Read my lips. Fix this problem! Then
          I'm calling in the feds and having you
          arrested for kidnapping.

                    JOE
          You knew how I felt about *Bambi*, and
          you let J.J. watch it anyway.

                    HARVEY
          You're going to the Big House, mister.
          You're doing time for morally
          corrupting my son.

                    JOE
          That's bullshit!

Harvey indignantly flips open the cell phone.

> HARVEY
> What do you call this naked tush?

> JOE
> She's not naked, she's in a thong.

> HARVEY
> I don't care what she wears on her
> feet!

> JOE
> Wake up and smell the Bengay. Your
> Gray Panthers out there is where
> Hector gets all his information.

> HARVEY
> How pathetic you are. Blaming
> helpless, innocent seniors.

Joe opens the blinds and points.

> JOE
> You know how Mary Jane got her
> nickname? She likes taking tokes . . .
> > (off Harvey's look)
> Smoking doobies . . . Mary Janes . . .
> pot . . . cannabis . . . weed . . .

> HARVEY
> *Liar!*

> JOE
> Of course, it's for medicinal
> purposes, but at her age—do the
> math . . . Willie over there has a
> stash of *Playboys* . . .

> HARVEY
> *Not true!*

> JOE
> His supplier works in food
> services . . .

> HARVEY
> *Liar! Liar!*

                    JOE
    I don't know who it is, but if it's
    the same guy who supplies Mary Jane,
    I'd check your brownies . . . Karl's
    addicted to Virgin Marys. He drinks
    hot sauce to kick in his endorphins.
    Keep tabs on your Tabasco . . . Oh,
    and last week Hector walked into the
    broom closet and caught Mr. Hanlan and
    Addie trying to get something going.

                    HARVEY
                 (he gasps)
    It's not true! . . . They can't have
    sex!

                    JOE
    They will now. Word's out he ordered
    Viagra.

                    HARVEY
    But they can't do that here!

                    JOE
    Why not?

                    HARVEY
    The man is eighty-three years old.

                    JOE
    Great, huh? He's working out, he's got
    good attitude, and now he's going to
    get a little.

                    HARVEY
    This is because of you! What if he
    can't take Viagra? What if he has a
    medical condition?

Conflict between the men moves every scene forward.

They pull medical records and call Casey. Hanlan's taking Nitro-Bid for a heart condition. At his age the drug interaction could be fatal.

Harvey loses it. Hanlan's going to die on his watch and they'll find Viagra in his system. Joe has the solution: they just won't let him get his hands on the stuff.

> HARVEY
> How do we do that?
>
> JOE
> We'll play suture ball. I'll keep it
> tame, but I'll physically get him
> exhausted. You go into his room and
> find it. After the game, we play some
> gut-wrenching movie like *The Notebook*.
> I don't watch chick flicks, but they
> say it sucks you dry. In the morning
> he won't remember he ordered Viagra.
> He won't even remember Addie.
>
> HARVEY
> What if it's not in his room?
>
> JOE
> . . . We need Hector.
>
> HARVEY
> Are you out of your mind! Why would I
> bring my son into this?
>
> JOE
> He knows the route of all the
> contraband.
>
> HARVEY
> Oh, God.
>
> JOE
> I'm telling you, your kid's out of
> control. It makes me question your
> parenting skills.
>
> HARVEY
> You raised a minutia freak! If
> something's a fraction off, it's like
> a tsunami hit. He single-handedly
> destroyed my garden.

```
                    JOE
        Yours tried to kill me with nachos and
        shellfish. Then he shot me off a roof
        and left me hanging nine hundred feet
        above the Las Vegas Strip.
```

Casey oversees the game. The action cuts between the suture ball on the field and Harvey searching Hanlan's room. Harvey finds the Viagra in the top drawer of the dresser. *The Notebook* plays for the seniors. The crying coming from the back of the room is Joe's. Casey explains to Harvey, he's still not over *Bambi*.

At the *act 2 turning point,* Hanlan's found dead. They find him, in the morning, collapsed over his dresser with his hands in his drawer. Harvey goes hysterical and insists Joe killed him! Casey is certain it's from natural causes. No, it's Joe! He's to blame for everything that's wrong in Harvey's life. It's been that way since he was seven.

Act 3, the resolution.

Here the characters have their biggest test. The stakes are raised to the highest pitch, and the action builds to the climax. Always ask yourself: Who is my character when the movie begins? What is the crisis that happens to him or her? How is the character changed in the end (the emotional arc)?

Again, we break the act into three units, running 7–10 pages each. We open on *unit 1*. It is less than a month later.

```
EXT. PADDLEWHEEL PARK — THREE WEEKS LATER

Joe is waiting on the bench. Harvey walks over and sits
down. Neither one of them looks at the other.
```

                    HARVEY
          Hector wants to spend the weekend with
          you. I am totally against it.

                    JOE
          J.J. wants the same thing. I can't talk
          him out of it.

                    HARVEY
          The only way my child is spending time
          with you is if I'm with him.

                    JOE
          You mean we spend time together?

                    HARVEY
          That or we go back to the judge.

                    JOE
          You or the bitch in the robe. Great
          choice.

They sit there in silence a long beat.

                    HARVEY
          You like to fish?

                    JOE
          Too slow . . . NASCAR races are coming up.

                    HARVEY
          The fumes are toxic . . . There's a
          home-and-garden show.

                    JOE
          Jesus, Harvey, can we do something
          without aprons? . . . Maybe a rodeo.

                    HARVEY
          I can't . . . Someday a cowboy's going
          to come down hard on a bronco and his
          big belt buckle is going to slice him
          in half.

                    JOE
          . . . A friend of mine knows some
          Yupik Eskimos who run a mushing camp.

Harvey slowly looks over.

                    JOE (CONT'D)
          What about dog sledding in Alaska?

                    HARVEY
          Are you out of your mind?

                    JOE
          These guys are Iditarod cham-
          pions. They do a deluxe safari
          thing . . . they even videotape the
          whole thing. It's a tame adventure.
          The boys would love it—the mountains,
          the pristine wilderness . . . huskies
          pulling us across the tundra . . . the
          cold clean air on our faces . . .

EXT. SEWARD ALASKA — DAY

A team of fourteen huskies pulling a sled with Joe,
J.J., Harvey, and Hector bundled up crossing the tundra.
The vistas are incredible. The driver, PUKAK, a Yupik
Eskimo, is driving the team.
They stop to make camp.
The boys watch Pukak unleash the huskies. He pets the
lead dog. In the b.g. a video has been has set up on a
tripod.

                    PUKAK
          His name's Hotfoot. When he was
          little, I could tell he'd be a leader.

                    J.J.
          What does *Pukak* mean?

                    PUKAK
          In Yupik, the translation is Snow
          Crust.

    While Pukak builds a fire, Joe, Harvey, and the boys play
on the ice. Joe surprises everybody with a giant inflatable movie
screen; he's failed though to read the small print; it's missing a
projector.

They eat caribou on the grill. Harvey plays video math with J.J. Joe teaches Hector blackjack. And all the while the giant movie screen sits against the barren tundra looking utterly ridiculous.

In every unit there is pivotal scene on which everything hinges: In unit 1, there is the bonding scene. That night the foursome sit in a circle and share a talking stick. Whoever takes the stick, Pukak explains, must share a message from his heart. The boys are sheepish at first, but admit they're glad they found a brother and the idea of having two dads isn't so bad after all.

Joe and Harvey, with a little help from Pukak's "herb tea," reveal more of themselves. Harvey confides there are times he still feels like the kid frozen in the center of the circle, unable to get out of his own way. Joe admits he doesn't let people get close. Friends send him self-help books and he's never cracked one open. "How can you change if you don't know what you want?" he asks. But for some weird reason right now is the happiest he's ever been.

Later, as the boys sleep, the men laugh and drink late into the night, reminiscing about their school days.

All seems right with their world and then—

In *unit 2*, we pull the carpet out from under them, putting more obstacles in their way to amp the action and build to turning point 2.

```
EXT. CAMPSITE — EARLY MORNING

The pristine silence is broken by the sound of blowers.
Harvey sticks his head out of the tent. Joe is trying to
suck the air out of the movie screen.
Pukak, in the b.g., is getting breakfast ready.
```

The huskies are hitched.
Everybody's packed up. Pukak's tying the movie screen to
the back of the sled.

> HARVEY
> We're taking that thing with us?

> JOE
> It's not deflating.
> > (off Harvey's look)
> Air Mall screwed me. I want a refund.

As Harvey gets into the sled, we notice the video cam
attached to the front. Joe removes a bottle he's been
hiding and hands it to Pukak. It's a fifth of Scotch.

> JOE
> This is for all your hard work. It's
> sherry-cask Scotch. The best, man.

THE TUNDRA — MOVING WITH THE SLED

The morning sun with unbroken vistas, the boys howling
like wolves, Harvey and Joe with alpha grins, and Pukak,
behind them, polishing off his fifth of Scotch.

> HARVEY
> Just man and the elements.

> JOE
> The way it's supposed to be, huh, Harvey?

> HARVEY
> This is it, Joe, the last frontier.

While sledding on the tundra Pukak hits a snow-bar, flies
out of the cab, bounces off the movie screen, and
disappears off screen. It's not until twenty minutes
later that they realize the huskies are leading them
without a driver.

The boys search the cab for a GPS and find the empty bottle. Harvey goes hysterical when he learns Joe gave their driver

Scotch. They're going to die like the Donner party. They're all going to freeze to death, if the bears don't eat them first. They'll find them all frozen in a glacier a thousand years from now like Otzii the Iceman! "Tame adventure my ass!" The boys eye Joe. Using their Boy Scout survival training, they pin Harvey to the ground and keep him there until he can get a grip on himself.

INT. COURTROOM — SEATTLE — DAY

Joe and Harvey stand before the same judge. Casey is seated in the gallery.

> JUDGE
> Good for the Boy Scouts. Why are you back here?

> HARVEY
> Your Honor, this man has shown signs of erratic, pernicious behavior since the age of seven.

> JUDGE
> Is this leading to something, or do you just hate the legal system?

> HARVEY
> He shows poor judgment. He knowingly placed me and my children into a vehicle with a drunk driver.

> JUDGE
> That's a serious offense, Mr. Connelly. Do you care to respond?

> JOE
> The vehicle was a sled, Your Honor. I couldn't see that the driver was drunk—he was behind us. All I could see were the huskies.

> JUDGE
> Where exactly were you?

                    HARVEY
     . . . Somewhere in the Arctic.

                    JUDGE
     Did you order your drunken sleigh
     driver to stop?

                    JOE
     No, he disappeared.

                    JUDGE
     What do you think happened to him?

                    JOE
     We don't know, Your Honor.

                    HARVEY
     I know! I have it all on videotape.
     You gave him Scotch, he hit a bump,
     and in his drunken stupor he bounced
     into the air and ricocheted off your
     ridiculous inflatable movie screen!
     His name was Pukak, Your Honor. In
     Yupik, the translation means Snow
     Crust. That's probably what he is
     right now. They won't find his body
     until spring.

                    JOE
     I'm sure Pukak is fine.

                    HARVEY
     Where is he, Joe? In Aruba sunning
     himself?
                    (to the judge)
     I want a restraining order keeping
     this man away from my son. We could
     have all died because of him.

                    JOE
     We could have all died because you
     panicked. Your Honor, I want the
     restraining order! In an emergency my
     son would not be safe with this man.

                    HARVEY
     You'll never change. You'll always be
     irresponsible!

                    CASEY
Your Honor, may I have a word?

                    JUDGE
Who are you?

                    CASEY
A character witness.

                    JUDGE
For whom?

                    CASEY
For both of them.

                    JUDGE
Then sit down. I don't trust you.

                    JOE
Milquetoast!

                    HARVEY
Maniac!

                    JOE
Pussy!

                    HARVEY
Womanizer!

                    JOE
Wuss!

                    JUDGE
That's it! I've had it with you two.
I'm placing restraining orders on both
of you. You're not allowed within five
hundred feet of each other, or the
children. Is that understood? Your
visitation rights are hereby revoked.

                    JOE/HARVEY
But . . . Your Honor . . .

                    JUDGE
You can contest it, but you'll have
a long legal battle on your hands.
                    (MORE)

```
                    JUDGE (CONT'D)
          For now, those boys are better off
          away from the mess you've created.


    Joe and Harvey exchange glances.
```

Joe and Harvey get what they ask for, and more. Now they are barred from seeing the boys they've grown so attached to.

In *unit 3,* the pain of separation brings insights to both men. Harvey's crocuses start to bloom. Joe starts reading self-help books. Neither man is happy, both are forced to start taking a hard look at themselves.

In the following scene we see changes starting to take place in Joe.

```
    INT. RESTAURANT — DAY

    Joe and Casey are at lunch.

                    CASEY
          Both boys called me. They want to see
          each other. I can pick them up and
          take them somewhere. You and Harvey
          don't have to have contact.

                    JOE
          If he's okay with it, it's okay by me.

                    CASEY
          What about Saturday? I'll take J.J.
          home, and you can have the night free.

                    JOE
          I don't want it free. I told J.J. I'd
          take him to the movies. You want to come?

                    CASEY
              Sure.
```

                        JOE
        . . . So, how is Harvey?

                      CASEY
        I don't know. I haven't seen him.

                        JOE
        Really? Then he's a bigger schmuck
        than I thought.

                      CASEY
                    (she shrugs)
        So, I'll pick J.J. up around noon.

                        JOE
        . . . Casey, I've been doing a lot
        of thinking . . . And I have feelings
        for you.

                      CASEY
        I have feelings for you.

                        JOE
        It's more than that. I really want you.

                      CASEY
        That's because I'm the only woman you
        haven't had.

                        JOE
        I think I'm in love with you.

                      CASEY
        I know you love me, Joe, but as a
        friend. You're getting the two mixed up.

                        JOE
        Why do you think that?

                      CASEY
        Because I know us. If we fell in love,
        we wouldn't have to do the work. We
        know each other too well. It would be
        safe and comfortable. I don't think
        it's supposed to be that easy for us.
        There are times I've thought about
        being with you, but it's always in
        panic mode, when I'm afraid nobody
        will ever love me and I'll die alone.

                          JOE
          Gee, thanks.

                        CASEY
          Come on, that's where you are right
          now. I like what we have. You do too.

                          JOE
          I thought I finally had something
          figured out . . . like I was making
          progress. Harvey was right. I'll never
          change.

                        CASEY
          Don't be so hard on yourself.

                          JOE
          This screw up is because of me. I
          don't think things through, and the
          people I care about get hurt. The kids
          miss each other, we miss the kids, and
          they think we're idiots. I even miss
          Harvey . . . These books I'm reading
          are starting to freak me out.

He leans in so no one can hear him.

                      JOE (CONT'D)
          These crying jags? Maybe there's too
          much estrogen in my system. It scares
          me big-time. I'm starting to lose my
          sex drive.

                        CASEY
          Maybe you're starting to care who you
          sleep with.

                          JOE
          That too.

Joe's working on himself. He's also starting to take responsibility for his actions.

In *unit 2*, he gets emotional watching the vacation tape, and he also puts his ego aside and advises Casey on how to put the moves on Harvey. He'll never make the moves on her, so she has to be the aggressor. She needs to grab him by the collar, drag him into the bedroom, strip him down fast, shove him on the bed, and jump his bones.

In the poignant scene between Harvey and Hector, it's his son who prompts his change.

```
INT. HARVEY'S BEDROOM — NIGHT

Harvey is lying in bed staring up at the ceiling. Hector
comes in.

                    HECTOR
          Dad? I can't sleep.

Hector gets in bed with him. They lie there a moment.

                    HECTOR
          Do you think Mom would get hurt if I
          didn't remember her much?

                    HARVEY
          No, you were very young.

                    HECTOR
          I remember some stuff.

                    HARVEY
          She was crazy about you . . . She was
          pretty, she loved to laugh . . . She
          was very exuberant.

                    HECTOR
          What's exuberant?

                    HARVEY
          Full of life . . . She'd walk into a
          room and the whole place would light
          up. Everybody wanted to be with her
          because she was so much fun.
```

                    HECTOR
          Kinda like Joe.

                    HARVEY
          Yeah. We were very different, but she
          liked that. She always said it
          balanced us out. . . . I loved
          her very much.

                    HECTOR
          It's hard losing the people you love.
          I miss Joe.

                    HARVEY
          I know you do.

                    HECTOR
          I thought it would be totally cool to
          have a whole lot of girlfriends like
          him, but he doesn't seem any happier
          than you. Maybe one is enough, if it
          was somebody cool like Casey. I think
          she likes you.

                    HARVEY
          Really?

                    HECTOR
          If you want something, you've got to
          declare yourself. That's what Joe
          says. He calls her a thoroughbred. He
          says any man that doesn't know it is a
          dumbass.

And we hold on Harvey a very long beat—

INT. CASEY HOUSE — MORNING

The doorbell rings. Casey, in a terrycloth robe and wet
hair, comes to the door.

                    CASEY
          Who is it?

                    HARVEY (O.S.)
          . . . It's Harvey.

```
                    CASEY
         . . . I just got out of the shower.
         Can you wait a minute?

                    HARVEY (O.S.)
         . . . No.

Casey reluctantly opens the door. He stands there a
moment staring at her, then steps in, passionately
kisses her, unties her robe, carries her to the bedroom,
drops her on the bed, and ravishes her.


INT. JOE'S HOUSE — SAME TIME

J.J., who's ready for school, picks up his tuba case and
is almost out the door.

                    J.J.
         Dad, your pill is on the counter.

                    JOE (O.S.)
         I already took it.

Joe comes out of the bedroom holding a pair of dirty
boxer shorts.

                    JOE
         What's this?

                    J.J.
         Oh yeah, my dirty shorts.

                    JOE
         I don't care about that; all I ask
         is that you pick them up. . . . Go,
         you're going to be late for school.
```

The *climax* of the script. Harvey breaks out of his shell. Like Joe, he changes. He has to, because what's at risk, he has learned, is more valuable.

INT. STRIKE SPORTS — JOE'S OFFICE — DAY

Joe's seated with the two male PGA execs we met earlier.
They are interrupted on the intercom. This was not
supposed to happen.

                    JOE
          Excuse me.

He walks to his desk.

                    JOE
               (under his breath)
          I said no interruptions.

                    HARVEY (O.S.)
          Do you think I'm spineless, Joe?

                    JOE
          . . . Harvey?

                    SECRETARY (O.S.)
          Sir, you can't go in there.

Harvey bursts in.

                    HARVEY
          I'm breaking the law, Joe. I'm
          committing a criminal offense. I could
          serve time for this. You're not
          looking at a scared little kid frozen
          in the circle anymore!
               (he dials)
          I'm calling the police . . . How's
          this for a milquetoast? . . . Hello?
          My name is Harvey Newman . . . I have
          breached a restraining order. I'm
          unarmed and on the tenth floor of
          Strike Sports, West Maple and Third.
          Come and get me.
               (hangs up)
          No backbone, huh, Joe? I don't care
          about the consequences. Do you know
          why? Because it was more important for
          to me to come down here and tell you
          that I love you.

                         JOE
                    (to the men)
          This isn't what it looks like.

                       HARVEY
          We are a family. I don't care if it's
          dysfunctional. We balance each other.
                    (pointing to pictures)
          These are our boys. They're brothers,
          for God's sake! They belong to both of
          us, and I'll be damned if I'm going
          to lose either one of them! . . . Or
          you! As Hector puts it, "It sucks when
          you're not around." So screw the law!

Joe stands there with his mouth open.

                         JOE
          I know balls . . . my friend, and
          you've got them.

Harvey can't hide that he's proud of himself.

                       HARVEY
          Yeah?

                         JOE
          Oh, yeah, big cojones.

He spots a picture of Casey.

                       HARVEY
          And this is my woman. Stay away from
          her!

                         JOE
          I'm cool with it. I'm happy for both
          of you.
                    (to the men)
          I love this guy. Look at me, and I'm not
          even crying.

And as the men watch, they embrace.

The *tag* or wrap-up of the screenplay (scenes following the climax) should run no longer than three to five pages. Anything longer kills the overall impact. In *Daddy*, it's two short scenes that end on a twist.

INT. COURTROOM — DAY

Harvey stands before the same judge in handcuffs. Joe is beside him. Casey and the boys are in the gallery.

                JOE
      Your Honor, I drop any and all charges
      against this man. He never posed a
      threat. We all love him . . .

                JUDGE
      I'm so sick of you people I could
      scream.

DISSOLVE TO:

ONE YEAR LATER

INT. CHURCH — DAY

CLOSE ON: Joe and Harvey. They are in tuxes. The altar is behind them. The wedding march begins to play.

WE PULL BACK

A four-year-old flower girl comes down the aisle. She passes Pukak, who we see seated among the guests. Another flower girl follows her. She can't be more than six. And still another; she's eight at the most. Hector and J.J., the ring boys, follow the girls out—and then comes Casey, smiling broadly. But to our surprise, she takes her place as the maid of honor.

THE BRIDE APPEARS

It is Lauren, mother of three and Las Vegas showgirl, who takes her place beside a beaming Joe.

INSERT — A SPORTS TABLOID

THE BOLD PRINT READS: *Strike Sports promotes sales exec, Joe Connelly, father of five* . . .

EXT. PARK — DAY

AS THE CREDITS ROLL:

The Newmans and the Connellys picnic. Hector and J.J. play and run around like banshees, teasing their sisters. Casey and Lauren are chatting, laying the food out. Joe and Harvey play Frisbee.

FREEZE FRAME

CRAWLER OVER THE CREDITS:

> The State of Washington granted Joe
> Connelly and Harvey Newman joint
> custody of the boys. Hector and J.J.
> now swap dads every other weekend.
>   The families all vacation
> together. Their next tame adventure is
> spelunking in the Adirondacks.
>   The AARP has officially recognized
> "touch" suture ball as "a healthy
> recreation for seniors."
>   Mr. Hanlan has a plaque at Sunset
> Rest Home honoring him as the "Father
> of the Double Fogie."

```
                    Pukak has been dry for a year.
                    Joe wants more children.


FADE OUT.


                         THE END
```

THE MOVIE OF THE WEEK: THE SEVEN-ACT STRUCTURE

Movies of the week run around ninety-five pages and consist of seven acts, with the exception of Lifetime movies, which have eight acts, the last being a quick wrap-up of the story.

But never write a spec M.O.W. script that is broken down into seven acts or eight acts. Instead, write a spec movie script (feature film or cable) that can be marketed to television. If a TV network exec spots a movie that fits his agenda, the fact that it's not broken down into acts will not hurt your chances for a sale.

Since there is little difference between cable movies and low-budget features, many two-hour scripts are marketed in both areas. By breaking your material down into seven acts, or eight acts, you are limiting yourself to only TV. There are hundreds of independent producers looking for small movies. Why do yourself a disservice and cut yourself off from this market? If the networks reject your script, you have absolutely nowhere else to take it: you can't take your TV movie and try to pass it around as a feature film script. Once readers spot seven acts, a lightbulb goes on that flashes *TV*, and they are automatically turned off by your project.

At this point, CBS and NBC have quit making movies of the

week. Showtime has cut back on its movie schedule, and USA, on the heels of its immense success with *The Starter Wife,* is focusing on series, as is HBO.

As a producer shopping other writers' projects, and as an episodic TV writer who, like many, made the transition to long form when TV movies were hot, this is disappointing news. But CEOs come and go, and agendas change.

The good news is, Lifetime, Hallmark, MTV, Nickelodeon, VH1, the History Channel, TNT, Oxygen, the Sci-fi Channel, and Disney are all making movies for their channels. These are generally low-budget, made for three million dollars or less.

Two movies I wrote as features sold to TV, one to ABC and another to Showtime. On both there were script changes. There are always script changes. This goes for all of television, not just M.O.W.'s, and for cable. Everybody gets their finger in the pie. It's a fact of the industry. There will be story meetings where you can negotiate some of the script changes, or make suggestions, but the writer must be willing to make concessions. Some of the suggested changes you may like; others you may hate. It is always in your best interest to be grateful you are working, implement what they want the best you can, and pray that their requests aren't outrageous.

My agent told me of a writer who sold a spec feature to television. The story was about a young man whose father gets hit in the head, goes crazy, and lands in a mental institution. The boy tries to bring his father back to reality and is ultimately forced to break into the institution, take his father, and run away with him. The network decided the boy should be a girl, the institution should be a prison, and the father should be crippled instead of crazy.

A marketing tip: if you are asked by an indie producer, or an agent, to write or break down your script into seven or eight acts, ask why. Who is the buyer, why is it necessary, and if they pass, where are we shopping the script next?

A writer in one of my workshops wrote an excellent thriller. At the time it met every parameter that Lifetime was looking for, except it was male-driven. On the encouragement of an indie producer, she decided to make her protagonist a female. I told her it was a lot work for one submission, and it would be harder than she anticipated. It was, but she pulled it off. The story changed in the process: it actually became better. The producer submitted it to Lifetime and they passed. When the script went out to other markets, it got more passes because it had a female lead. Writers should always save all of their drafts!

Some producers throw handfuls of projects against a wall to see what sticks. Writers are the ones who put in all the work. Ask questions and weigh in. If the answers feel good to you, then go for it, but never be afraid to ask.

Let's look briefly at the seven-act breakdown. If we place seven acts into the basic three-act structure, they would be divided for the most part as they are in figure 2. (*Note*: These acts *are* delineated and placed on the page.)

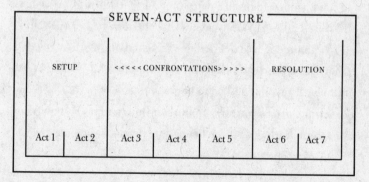

Figure 2.

A movie of the week runs about ninety-five pages. If these acts consisted of equal lengths, they would run about thirteen or fourteen pages. Knowing this helps the writer keep track of the page count, but the acts don't break down evenly, they stagger. Act 1 is almost always longer because there is more to establish. It can run up to twenty pages; another act can run as short as nine.

Each act is a narrative chunk or unit that builds to an act end leading to a commercial break. As in all TV, the act end is a mini climax, and now we are structuring around seven of them.

Pamela Wallace (Academy Award winner for *Witness*) and I had previously collaborated on *If the Shoe Fits*, a feature starring Rob Lowe and Jennifer Grey. Once when she was visiting, we came up with an idea: What if you got a wrong-number phone call from someone who sounded very attractive? What if the person then called you back and you began a conversation with him? It was an interesting springboard so we took it one step further. People will confide things to perfect strangers that they might never tell their most intimate friends.

The result was *Alibi*—an erotic thriller. The log line was: A ski champ, laid up after an accident on the slopes, receives a wrong-number phone call from a software tycoon. The two hit it off and become intimate phone friends—until his wife is murdered and the skier realizes that she may be his only alibi.

With the log line defined, we sketched out what we needed to have happen in each act. Writers work differently. What we do, and what I recommend, is to begin with a very broad overview of each act, just as we did with the half-hour and hour show, with everything leading to the act end. The details happen later.

. . .

Act 1: Marti's downhill race and accident. She's laid up and bored. Her fiancé manager is always gone. She gets the phone call. The man calls her back. They begin friendly chats that turn highly erotic. The man never identifies himself, which titillates her. She goes to a lingerie shop where he has a gift waiting for her.

Act 1 end: On the phone that night he tells her in detail every move she made in the dressing room. She knows she's being watched.

Act 2: We reveal the caller. He is Connor Hill, the president of a high-tech computer firm, who makes his calls to Marti from his penthouse office. While they are on the phone, there is a commotion outside. Connor takes an interrupt call and tells Marti something terrible has happened.

Act 2 end: Connor's wife and partner in the company is found strangled in the parking garage.

Act 3: Connor is brought in for questioning. Marti recognizes his voice on TV. This is the man she has been talking to. She knows he's innocent: at the time of the murder she was on the phone with him. She confronts Connor. Their sexual attraction is even more powerful in person. Connor can afford the best attorneys. He does not want Marti to come forward. There is too much at stake for her.

Act 3 end: The cliffhanger. Marti faces a moral dilemma. Will she do the right thing, come forward, destroy her relationship, and ruin her reputation? She is Connor's only alibi.

. . .

The action now shifts around into the second hour:

Act 4: Marti takes the stand for Connor. It's revealed in court that Connor's wife was having an affair. All the evidence begins pointing to her lover. Connor pursues Marti while the trial is going on. She struggles with her feelings and tells him to stay away.

   Act 4 end: She sexually caves in.

Act 5: The relationship becomes intensely physical. Marti is cornered by the victim's lover, who tells her Connor set him up.

   Act 5 end: At Connor's house, Marti discovers a list of women's names and phone numbers. The first names are scratched off, hers is at the bottom with a checkmark next to it.

Act 6: Marti tries to track down the women on the list. Only one can be reached. She vaguely recalls a wrong caller. The man called her back and tried to make conversation with her.

   Act 6 end: Connor gets acquitted. The police officer, who throughout the story has been trying to get evidence on him, warns Marti to be careful. Connor does not need her anymore.

Act 7: At a victory celebration at Connor's company, Marti slips off by herself and finds an engineer working on a computer program. She learns the company is developing artificial intelligence for military applications. The engineer has her talk to the computer, and the computer can respond to her in any voice it is given.

   Connor interrupts them. He has a surprise for Marti. He is taking her away to his Aspen lodge as a thank-you for all she has done. Everything has been taken care of, and the plane is waiting.

In Aspen, on a desolate mountaintop, Marti learns the truth. She accesses Connor's computer and finds a "voice box," and clicks it. She hears a conversation between the two of them. He walks in on her. She confronts him. He wasn't on the phone when his wife was murdered; she was talking to a computer program. It was all planned, even down to picking the right woman on the telephone.

Act 7 end (climax): There is no way off the mountain for Marti except on skis. Connor, an expert skier, grabs a gun and takes out after her. She leads him down an off-line trail of rocks and cliffs. She finds a treacherous jump; a miscalculation here and there is no way a person could survive. She waits for him, hidden. At the moment he makes his jump, she uses her poles to push him off balance and he falls to his death.

With the general overview and the act ends clear, we now had our roadmap. We were then able to go back and begin structuring our scenes.

WHAT IS MEANT BY *HIGH CONCEPT*?

The term *high concept*, a catchphrase used throughout the industry, refers to an idea with a strong hook that has broad audience appeal. A high concept can be communicated in one or two short simple sentences.

A number of years after *Alibi* aired, Pam was having lunch with a friend who told her an incredible true story. She was very

young and had just opened her law practice when she was vis-
ited by an odd man who needed a defense attorney to represent
him in a murder trial. She asked for the specifics, and he told her
the murder had not yet been committed. He was going to kill his
wife's lover. She was at a loss as to what to do. She was hoping
the man wouldn't return, but he did—twice—and made numerous phone calls, insisting she was his attorney. He told her that
if she went to the police, she would be breaking attorney-client
privilege. She went to the ex-wife and her lover to warn them,
and discovered the lover was her former boyfriend! The attorney did go to the police, but they did very little to help her. The
man continued to harass her and eventually succeeded in killing
the lover. Today he's serving a life sentence.

Is this high concept? You bet! We got the rights to the story
and couldn't run to Showtime fast enough. We sold it and it was
put in development, and the script was *Murder with Privilege*.

Network executives believe that high concept, whether
comedy or drama, is synonymous with good ratings (although
we know this isn't always the case).

The difference between movies for television and feature
films is that movies for TV tend to rely exclusively on high
concepts or the sensational to pull in big ratings. The lineup of
network M.O.W.'s and cable movies for last year included *True
Confessions of a Hollywood Starlet*, *The Starter Wife*, *Fat Girl*,
and *Fat Like Me*, and from what I just learned from a producer
friend, a certain network is still looking for fat stories. Evidently
fat is big right now.

In a few months this will change, so try not to write for a
trend, because you'll find yourself behind the wave. One year

they wanted depth and inspiration, and last year they wanted fluff. I almost fell out of my chair when I got a call looking for WWII scripts and female westerns. I even got a call from an exec to whom I had pitched a sci-fi with my partner from NASA. At the time she had no interest in the project whatsoever, but then when the Mars Rover was getting all the attention, she called me up and wanted to know if the script was still available! My point is, never throw anything out.

High concept also applies to feature films, where the term has become synonymous with big box-office hits: *Liar Liar*, *Analyze This*, *What Women Want*, *Lethal Weapon*, *Die Hard*, *I Am Legend* are just some examples. The list is endless.

For movies for cable television and feature films, your best shot for a sale is with a high-concept script—or at least for your first script going in. This is not to say you should compromise the quality of your writing. The scripts mentioned above were all very well written. It is what the market thrives on: just turn to the movie page in your newspaper or open the *TV Guide*. Know it, consider it, then write what you must. There have always been those bold, creative souls who break from the commercial and write a hit, or whose material is so special it finds its way to a champion who gets it produced. Those writers are my heroes.

But a story about a poor British coal miner's son who wants to be a ballet dancer, or a puppeteer who discovers a portal into the head of John Malkovich, or a sweet, shy man who has a deep, meaningful relationship with a sex doll he's ordered off the Internet is a very tough sale. *Billy Elliot*, *Being John Malkovich*, *Lars and the Real Girl*, *Little Miss Sunshine*, and *Sideways* (and we could go on and on) are niche gems that took years to get made, showed at festivals and in art houses, and spread by word of mouth.

One of the biggest complaints among producers today is that scripts lack passion. In the end, you are the only guide. Let your passion dictate; listen to your inner self. You must care about your subject and it will show on the pages.

The Story of Vera Blasi, Screenwriter

Vera Blasi was born in São Paulo, Brazil. Her father was Lebanese. After he died, her mother remarried and the family moved to New York. Vera came into my six-month workshop after graduating from Notre Dame College, where she studied literature and arts. I keep this screenwriting workshop small and run it to resemble the development process in Hollywood; writers in the workshop develop their screenplays over a six-month period and get them ready for market. It's a wonderful opportunity for a teacher because it allows you to really get to know the writer's work. And Vera's was very good. She was there for a year.

Vera wrote about the things she knew, like coming to America and settling in Manhattan, with no knowledge of the language, as a twelve-year-old child. She was multicultural and had unique stories. Stories of Fatima and angels held fascination for her, not because she was religious, but because there was a bit of the mystic in her.

One of the best things about Vera was her mother's cooking. Vera was living at home at the time, and whenever we voted on where we would next meet, it was always at Vera's house. The food was unbelievable; it was like magic. You could not help falling in love with any woman who could cook like this.

Vera's writing was wonderful, but I was told it was too soft, that it wasn't commercial enough and that softness would be her downfall. Maybe she heard it too.

I'll never forget the day she walked into class with a kick-ass, AK-47, blow-your-guts-out, blood-flying-everywhere first thirty pages of a screenplay. Everybody read it and we sat there with our mouths open. It was very well written, but it wasn't Vera. It didn't have her unique voice. It was Hollywood talking.

Vera got accepted to AFI, the American Film Institute. I am proud to say I wrote one of her recommendation letters. We talked periodically after that, and then we lost contact for a while.

One day I was watching a great little film about a young, beautiful woman from a small town in Brazil whose cooking was so delicious that it was magical. The woman, harassed by a chauvinist husband, moves to San Francisco and becomes a renowned TV chef. Something was feeling a little familiar about the places and people in this story. Some of the dishes the Brazilian chef was preparing I had eaten before. The movie was *Woman on Top*, starring Penelope Cruz, and the writer was Vera Blasi.

Vera wrote what she knew about. She wrote from a place of passion. She found her voice, what made her unique, and wasn't deterred from using it.

I doubt that AK-47, blow-your-guts-out script ever made it past page thirty.

After *Woman on Top*, Vera Blasi went on to write the movie *Tortilla Soup* and is currently scripting *The Lions of Al-Rassan* from a novel by Guy Gavriel Kay, for Bedford Falls and director Edward Zwick. This is very big project. Bravo, Vera!

12.

DEVELOPING THE
TWO-HOUR MOVIE

STEP 1: DEFINING THE SPINE

If you can't define it, you can't write it! The *spine* is the central idea or core of the story. I call it the spine because it is what everything hinges on. It is what the story is about.

This is a story about a spoiled sorority blonde who gets dumped by her boyfriend and manages to get herself into Harvard Law School to win him back. (*Legally Blonde*)

This is a story about a lost alien who is befriended by a young boy who helps him find his way back home. (*E.T.*)

This is a story about a pregnant sixteen-year-old girl who decides to have her baby and seek out good parents for it. (*Juno*)

Inherent within all of the spines above are character, need, conflict, and action.

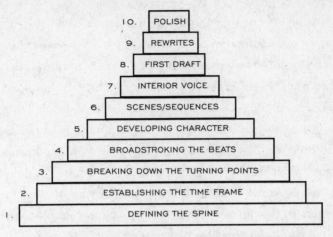

BUILDING BLOCKS OF THE TWO-HOUR MOVIE
Figure 3.

Too often, producers and studio execs complain, "somewhere along the way screenwriters get off track. They forget what they are writing about."

While writing and developing your screenplay, repeat to yourself over and over: ***This story is about***. This will help you stay on track.

STEP 2: ESTABLISHING THE TIME FRAME

Does your story take place in one night? Over the span of the football season? In the movie *The Holiday*, two women in different countries swap houses for two weeks, meet local men, and fall in love. *Atonement* is an epic that spans several decades. *Into the Wild* follows the free-spirited Christopher McCandless over an adventurous and doomed two-year journey.

In an interview for *Written By*, the Writers Guild of America, West, magazine, writer-director Tony Gilroy talked about his on-again, off-again struggle with the movie *Michael Clayton*. He pushed the project aside for two years and kept coming back to it. He said he suddenly realized one day that he didn't even know how many days the film took place in. It was insane. He had been writing for fifteen years and he didn't know the time frame? What was he doing? So he made a decision: if he didn't at least know that by the end of the week, he was dropping the project. By the end of the day he had it: the story took place over four days. Within three weeks, he had finished the script.

A movie is a series of fragments, a blueprint of visual impressions that give the illusion of a complete story when strung together. By defining the time frame, the writer identifies the right fragments needed to tell the story. A vague time frame leads to poor decisions and no guardrails to keep you from going off structure.

STEP 3: BREAKING DOWN THE TURNING POINTS

Attempting to write without knowing where you are going is no better than driving around blindly looking for a house when you could ask for directions. This step is simply identifying where you want to go. (See Chapter 11.)

- What is your page 10 hook?
- What happens at the act 1 end? (turning point 1)
- What happens at midpoint?

- What happens at the act 2 turning point?
- How does your story end?

Once you know where you're going, you can map out the best way to get there.

STEP 4: BROADSTROKING THE BEATS

These are not detailed beats; they are beats that are crucial to the story, like beats needed in the heart to keep it pumping. Imagine yourself telling a story to a group of adolescents. You're telling them the setup to the story *Splash*. You need to keep it simple—so simple, in fact, that if you left out one beat, the story wouldn't work. What are the story beats you must hit?

- A young boy on a Cape Cod ferry with his brother and his parents impulsively dives overboard.
- He is saved by a beautiful young girl—a mermaid.
- We pick him up sixteen years later. He runs a New York produce company, his brother is a playboy ne'er-do-well, and his girlfriend is leaving him because he can't say "I love you."
- He gets drunk after a wedding and impulsively takes a cab to Cape Cod.
- He hires a boat to take him to the other side of the island. There is a boating accident. Once again he is saved by the mermaid, now sixteen years older. She

deposits him on land. He yells for her to stay, but she disappears.

- The mermaid finds his wallet with his address in the water.
- She arrives in Manhattan, trades in her fins for a pair a legs, and is spotted standing naked at the Statue of Liberty. Police arrest her.
- At the police station, the cops call the name on the wallet. Our hero and mermaid are brought together.

There are wonderful details and very funny moments in the setup to *Splash*. We meet Alan Bauer on the ferry with his family. His younger brother is throwing coins on the deck so he can look up women's skirts.

When the script picks him up sixteen years later, Alan is having a very bad day. His produce is looking bad this season, and a vendor is giving him a hard time. His secretary has been struck by lightning and is wearing her brassiere on the outside of her clothes. His girlfriend calls and says she's moving out. A car crashes into a stack of fruit carts and his brother gets out excitedly waving a magazine. His article, "Lesbian No More," got published in *Penthouse* magazine!

This is all fabulous stuff, but it's detail. I tell writers to leave it out for another step. If something wonderful occurs to you, jot it down and go back to the business at hand. This is your structure. You want this sheet as clean and uncluttered as possible.

The broadstroking for the entire script can be stepped out in two or three pages.

STEP 5: DEVELOPING CHARACTER

Structure holds the story in place, but it's character, scene by scene, line by line, that takes you through the script. Once you have determined the spine, time frame, and beats of the story, the character/characters, if fully developed, will tell you how to go the rest of the way.

Underdeveloped protagonist/protagonists result in a one-dimensional script, whereas intense character work not only opens up the screenwriter visually but also develops other aspects of the script. The people in your character's personal life and professional life become characters in your story. Their routines and the places they frequent become your locales. *Character development* does not *have to wait until step 5.* Some screenwriters may choose the character step before they identify the turning points, or even the spine of the story. It is crucial, however, that character work is completed before step 6. If you put time into developing your characters, they will drive the story, not your plot. They will tell you where to go.

STEP 6: SCENES/SEQUENCES

With the character work now complete, step out the scenes and/or sequences connecting the beats to the plot points. You already know your destination; in the step process you decide how to get there.

Identifying sequences is an incredibly helpful tool when working with screenplays. It's like finding chunks of your movie.

The wedding sequence in *The Godfather* ran forty minutes. There was the big Italian celebration for Connie and Carlo; the Godfather agreeing to do a favor for Bonasera the mortician with a caveat in return; Sonny having sex with a woman who was not his wife; Michael, in uniform, arriving with Kay; the big entrance with Johnny Fontane—every scene introduced us to the characters and served a purpose.

If a scene or sequence does not provide us with new, pertinent story information or character revelation, it is excess and does not belong in the script (see Chapter 8).

I tell writers it's unnecessary to have a detailed list of every locale and scene in the movie. If you feel you absolutely have to do this, then all of your planets are in Virgo and you're most likely single. Some scenes will come to you while you are writing, others you will remove, some you will combine. Allow yourself a little room to riff on the first draft.

When stepping out, ask yourself what needs to be established and list it. This will tell you if it can be written in single scene or it needs a sequence.

Many writers find it helpful to use index cards. Each card represents a scene or sequence. On the card is the locale, who is in the scene, and what needs to be established.

I have problems with the cards. They're impossible on planes, I'm constantly losing them, and they show up in weird places. Sleeping one night, my partner felt something hard underneath his ear. He felt around in his pillowcase and pulled out an index card that read, "Establish Hal as a cross-dresser."

STEP 7: INTERIOR VOICE

The interior voice is your inner picture, where you go inside the scene or sequence and become the filmmaker. Ask yourself here, What are the inner components that can make this scene work? Riff it. Use stream of consciousness and play with it. How do I establish what I need? How do I envision it? How can I make it interesting?

Let's say you've just stepped out *The Karate Kid*. In this particular scene Daniel's mother needs to discover his black eye. It's key to the story. How does it happen? What is she doing? What's Daniel doing? Ask yourself, What are the different ways it could play out?

Maybe it's morning. Maybe she's cooking breakfast. Daniel sneaks out of the bedroom wearing a giant pair of shades. He tries to get out unnoticed. She wants them to have breakfast together; he insists he has to go. She spots him as he is leaving and asks what's up with the shades. He makes a joke, and says, "It's California." She tells Daniel to sit down, but he makes more excuses. She's starting to get scared.

Finally, she demands he take off the glasses. He reluctantly exposes his shiner. She's horrified. Daniel lies and says it was a bicycle accident.

The above scene was constructed by screenwriter Robert Mark Kamen, and it worked beautifully in the movie.

There are many other ways this scene could have played out. No two writers have the same vision. See the pictures play out in your head. Hear the dialogue. Be in the audience for a while in your head and then jot down what you see on paper.

How you choose to do this is up to you. You may like out-lines or bullets. For many, writing in narrative prose is very help-ful. It frees up the writer and allows ideas to flow. There are no rules here. What is important is your vision. You can synopsize, outline, write on cards or Post-its. Find what works best for you.

Going inside the scene/sequence and expanding your vision is the most creative and satisfying part of structuring. You become the filmmaker; the movie becomes alive in your head. A great read is a visual experience. Screenwriters must see their movie visually before they can create it on the page.

STEP 8: FIRST DRAFT

The foundation has been laid, you've done all the groundwork: now you begin writing the script in format. Leave yourself some room here. As you write some scenes, you'll discover you don't need them at all, and others will need to be added. Better ideas will jump out at you, and others you'll look at and say, What was I thinking? Go with it, but don't veer off track. You know what your story is about; it's become your mantra.

What's most important in first draft is to get it down on paper. Don't let your inner critic get in the way. Perfection-ism leads to procrastination, which leads to paralysis—and the premature editing of a potential gem. Remember, the first draft exists to be rewritten.

Some of my best writers are the ones who get the most stuck. They set the bar very high for themselves, and when they don't hit it, they freeze. Because they're good, they feel the added pressure of turning in good pages. I tell them to just sit down and write poorly. Then, when they come out of cardiac arrest, I tell them what I do to get unstuck. I tell myself, "Today I'm not writing, I'm learning how to write." For some reason that frees me up. I get gutsier and start trying new things and experimenting. It helps get me out of myself.

On the first draft, if you've done the structure and the character work, and you know the scene needs to be there, and you know what has to be revealed, then what is the worst that can happen? You write poorly. First drafts exist to be rewritten.

STEP 9: REWRITES

Here, we trim, cut, and perfect our script. Corrections are made, the points are clarified and defined, the characters are intensified, and dialogue and narrative are tightened and sharpened. It is time for the inner critic to go to work. Great scripts happen in the rewriting. Be ruthless with your own material.

Somewhere in the rewriting process, I highly recommend a script consultant. Clean the script up as best you can, but don't try to get it to a polished state. A good consultant will have many notes, and that means rewrites. You're not paying a consultant to impress them; you're paying for their professional advice. Why add more rewrites than are necessary?

STEP 10: POLISH

I once asked an agent, "When do you know your script is ready to go out?" He said, "When you know you can't make it any better, it's the best you've got."

Don't send material out until it's ready. Many writers have made this mistake—including me. Give yourself a little time away from the script. Writers are so happy they're finally finished, they lose their perspective. Look at the script again in a couple of days and you'll get down on your knees and thank God you didn't hit the send button.

And no typos and formatting errors! Find a proofreader. Industry people get very annoyed with sloppy submissions. The script must look totally professional.

13.

ADAPTATIONS, COLLABORATIONS, AND MY BIGGEST MISTAKES

ADAPTATIONS

I've often been approached by new writers who want me to talk about adaptations. What if they could get their hands on a book and secure the film rights?

I've written a number of adaptations, and it's challenging to take existing material, especially books and novels, and translate them to film. It's a great exercise in what filmmaking is all about; in fact, I think it would make for a terrific class—choosing a novel, finding the movie inside it, and then structuring the screenplay.

My favorite adaptation was a collaboration with screenwriter Pamela Wallace for producer Ellen Freyer, on the Newbery Honor winner *Catherine, Called Birdy*, by Karen Cushman. It's about a feisty girl living in medieval England who fights off her father's choice of suitors. The screenplay was like a juvenile *Shakespeare in Love*, and writing it was great fun, like being back in classical theater during my college days. We sold the script to Ben Myron Productions. Unfortunately, the movie was tough to set up because it was a period piece, which means a big budget, and it had a young female lead, neither of which is a good bet. Ann Hathaway, who read for the producers, loved the Birdy character and almost came on board. *Almost* is a word you hear a lot in Hollywood.

I have friends in publishing, in the smaller houses, and we make a point of keeping in touch. I'm always in search of a good book. I also search the Web for self-published books. Around two years ago I came across a title I loved, *Undercover White Trash*. I read the book; it was very funny and I liked it a lot. I contacted the author David Kilpatrick and took an option out on it. The screenplay I wrote by the same title was optioned by Gimme a Break Productions.

I've found the authors I've worked with to be very cooperative. At first, some are a bit cautious, because of prior bad experiences with Hollywood. Sometimes their reasoning is legitimate, and sometimes it's just the nature of the industry. I find that once you build a rapport with the authors, and they feel they can trust you, they are very supportive.

About five years ago I walked into a bookstore and saw a very pretty blond woman signing children's books. She was Wendelin Van Draanen, the author of the Sammy Keyes series of novels, featuring a teenage detective named Samantha ("Sammy") Keyes. *Sammy Keyes and the Hotel Thief* won the 1999 Edgar

Allan Poe Award for Best Juvenile Mystery. We struck up a conversation and started communicating by phone. I read everything she had written, and I loved her work. The contact eventually led to my getting an option on *Sammy Keyes and the Hotel Thief*, with a pickup for three more books if a television series was made. I wrote the treatment for a backdoor pilot (a movie) and developed the bible with Wendelin for the TV series. We got a deal with an American-Canadian company, and Wendelin and I signed our part of the contract. The producer attached to the project, who had fought with tenacity to get us the deal, used the same tenacity holding out on the terms of her contract. After endless months of negotiating, the company got fed up and walked.

This is why authors get frustrated and writers get bitter. The Sammy Keyes series has gone on to become extremely successful. Wendelin is now on book fifteen of her twenty-book series and has a huge fan base of kids ages nine to fifteen. I'm happy to say that her book *Flipped*, now titled *Bro-Jitsu: The Martial Art of Sibling Rivalry*, is in development with Rosen-Obst Productions with Nora Ephron attached as the writer.

I've often been asked how one gets a book optioned. It depends on the book. Best sellers are out of the question. Even if you have the big bucks to obtain an option, agents and studios get the galleys before the books are released and tie up the rights. I have tried to get my hands on smaller books and often found the same holds true for them. But sometimes books do fall through the cracks.

You can search self-published books on the Internet, and also find smaller publishing houses that list their libraries.

If something interests you, it's very easy to find out about the movie rights. Simply call the publishing house and an operator will connect you to a tape recording with directions on where to write in or e-mail, and you will have your answer in a couple of weeks. I have also sought out authors through publishing houses by asking for their agent's name. Agents will contact their client for you, and if the author is interested, they will get back to you.

Never commit to writing anything until you know if the rights are available, no matter how old or obscure the book may be. Always get this information first.

COLLABORATIONS

This industry is not one in which you shine alone. Film and TV is a highly collaborative art form. At every stage of development, meetings are involved. Everybody has an opinion; there is always compromise.

Many scriptwriters collaborate in Hollywood also. Writing teams are very common. Throughout this book I have mentioned my various collaborative projects. Most of them have been great fun, but there are a few that have been difficult.

Writing alone has its advantages: egos aren't involved, you make more money, and the vision is all yours. But it gets lonely, and if you are social by nature, you may find that you are more creative and have more discipline when you are working with someone else.

If you are considering a writing collaboration, there are some very important issues you must address. Sharing the writing process is like walking down the aisle together. Both people are very trusting and idealistic at first, but as in a marriage, when difficulties arise, egos get involved and feelings get hurt. If there is not an open line of communication, the partnership can turn very sour. Nothing will kill the creative partnership faster, and breaking up can be as difficult as in a marriage.

If you choose to write with a partner, and the script sells, you are obligated to remain with that partner on your next assignment. Producers and story editors are buying a team, and they will not settle for half of it. If you build a career with your partner, then choose to break up, it will be like beginning all over again. For some inexplicable reason, the Hollywood mentality assumes whichever partner isn't in the room is the one who did all the work.

This problem is so prevalent that my agent jokingly told me once that writers should make prenuptial agreements. Writers should decide, in the event of a breakup, who will take credit for which script—sort of like divvying up the kids—and each should have permission from the other to take his or her name off the scripts they don't retain.

Once you're an established writer, it's easier to collaborate on different projects, because you have proven yourself and you have sole credits.

If you choose to work with a partner, if you are seriously writing to sell, and if you want to establish yourself as a team, here are the ground rules for building a successful collaboration.

1. Communication is key. You must trust each other's opinions. Listen, and be willing to compromise. Egos

must get out of the way. Everything has to be geared toward the good of the project.

2. Is the other writer as committed as you are? What if midway through the project he or she decides to quit, or decides to relocate? Will the rights revert to the writer who completes the project? Discuss the situation and get backup plans on paper. You don't need an attorney; you simply need an agreement between the two of you in writing.

3. How much time is your partner willing to invest in the project and the partnership? What about expenses? Writing is not a cheap proposition: there are copying fees, supplies, business lunches, and research expenses. Is your partner financially committed as well?

4. Decide whose name will go first. This point sounds trivial, but later it can become a big issue. Flip a coin, or maybe you should decide what sounds best. In any case, decide in the beginning.

5. Choose a partner who complements you, one who possesses strengths where you are weak, and vice versa. The point of a good partnership is that you write better faster. Two idea people can discount each other. The same is true of two organizers: they're like two positive sides of a magnet coming together. It is the differences between you and your partner that make for a powerful team.

6. Know the personal life of your partner. Writing takes a lot of time. In fact, you may spend more time with

your partner than with your spouse. With the many
hours spent together, the line between professional
and personal becomes very blurry. You both need
to know the commitment you've made and what it
will entail. Does this person have kids? What about a
spouse, boyfriend, or girlfriend: will they resent the
time you require? I once was approached by a doctor
who had a great idea for a medical mystery. It was very
annoying when his girlfriend started coming to our
meetings. After a while, I didn't know if it was just the
two of us writing, or me, the doc, and the nutcase from
Fatal Attraction. Needless to say, the project never
got off the ground. The good news is, I heard he was
finally able to break free of her. I pray no rabbit is boil-
ing in a pot somewhere!

7. Find out which of you has the most powerful verbal skills, and let that person be the "front" man or
woman. Two writers outtalking each other at a pitch
session just won't do. Let one do the talking and the
other chime in when necessary. One is the driver, the
other is a navigator.

8. Decide who will do what writing task and when. If
either of you falls short, the other should be able to
call the neglectful partner on it and pinch-hit.

9. Spend a week discussing your writing arrangements so
that before you begin, nothing is assumed and everything is clear.

10. When you begin writing, have everything stepped out
and know exactly where you're going with the story.

There should be no surprises. Everything should be decided between the two of you beforehand.

MY BIGGEST MISTAKES

Taking Notes Literally

Development executives can spot what doesn't work but are not always good at telling you how to make it work. Taking their notes too literally can sometimes be deadly to the writer. Case in point:

While working on a Disney half-hour animation piece, I was given notes by a development exec. I wanted to do a really good job for this woman, because this was new territory for me, and I wanted to impress her. I followed her notes to the T. Ideas occurred to me while I was writing, things I thought would work better, but I stopped myself. I did only what she asked for. When I turned the project in, she said she was disappointed. I asked her why. I had done everything she wanted. She said, "I know, but I expected more." From that day forward it was very clear to me that writers had to do more than just implement notes, they had to interpret them. I resolved never to take development notes that literally again.

At meetings, I'd jump into the conversation just to make sure I was clear. If I was wrong, we would talk it out together. If a thought came to me later that meant a significant change, I'd make a phone call and run it past the execs. Sometimes I'd just implement my idea and let them take the credit for it. If it's good, they usually do. If an idea doesn't work, it's always the writer's fault anyway.

Always Listening to My Agent

I was approached by a nonpro with a very thick book entitled *Grania*, by Morgan Llywelyn. This book was a terrible risk as a film. It was about the legend of Grace O'Malley, the warrior chieftain for the last tribe of Ireland, and her power struggle with Queen Elizabeth I. Each woman wanted what the other had. Grace, who was loved by her people, fought on the battlefield with her men and led a lusty life filled with lovers and children at her side, but she never possessed the power of Elizabeth. Elizabeth, with all her power, ruled from a distance. She envied the life of passion that Grace led.

Both women were amazing warriors. They were born in the same year and died in the same year, at eighty. Their respect grew great for each other. In her later years, when Grace was destitute and her tribe was dying, she took a famous trip down the Thames and proudly came to Elizabeth and asked for eighteen articles of provision to keep her tribe from perishing. Elizabeth granted her all of them.

I said to myself, "Okay, too expensive, too big, a period piece, some of it even on water, two female leads, and Academy Awards written all over it." My background was acting; I would have given my soul for one of these roles. What an opportunity for two great actresses to work together.

My agent told me I was an idiot to take an option out on the book. This made a lot of sense. I did it anyway.

With the help of two collaborators, one an authority on Queen Elizabeth, and the other an authority on paganism (O'Malley had a servant who taught her the old ways), we began whittling away at the book. We combined some characters, cut others out, and created a character that was really terrific. At the time, I was working on other projects, but it took us a total of about six months.

Then I went to work writing a twenty-page treatment. I knew there was no way in hell I would get the opportunity to write this script. This movie was too big. It would only go to an A-list writer.

My agent flipped out when she read the treatment. She loved it.

Through a contact of mine, the project somehow ended up in Helen Hunt's hands. I was home working one afternoon when she called me from her car and said she had to play the role of Grace.

Helen was with CAA; I was with a midsize boutique agency. I told my agent I was happy taking a producer credit. She told me to fight for first draft, that a producer credit meant nothing for my career. She was adamant. I knew this was a mistake.

But what if my agent was right? What if I did get first draft? They would bring in another writer to rewrite me anyway. But what if I did a great job? Maybe this could be my Academy Award too. Hell, I found this project. I was the one who sweated over it. I agreed, let's go for it. The fight went on too long. I finally came to my senses and said, "Take the damn producer credit!" By then it was too late, and Helen had moved on to another project. It was *As Good As It Gets* and she got her Academy Award anyway. We had a window of opportunity and we blew it.

I later came to find out that my agent and Helen's agent were related, so there was more going on here than just business. I was given poor advice, but I didn't have to listen to it. Writer's ego got the better of me. A producer credit would have been just fine. I should have taken it and been happy.

Not Listening to My Inner Voice

How does one explain something that has no logic?

I wrote a sci-fi feature with Jim Logan, my partner of sixteen years, who worked for NASA, about the first manned space colony, called Island One. In it were some adolescents who were great characters. A woman who was my workshop assistant thought these kids would make a great TV series. At the time, there was a big push for entertainment that was educational. I thought it was a great idea and said she should help us develop it. *Big mistake.* I should have said, "Thank you, and if by some remote chance this idea should ever sell, you will get a very nice check from us."

The idea became *Space Trackers*. The log line: *Five quirky school-age kids living in an international space colony fifty years in the future meet in a learning lab to study the dawn of the 21st century on Earth.*

I gave my assistant a shared "created by" credit and explained that her having no writing credits could possibly pose a problem down the line. My partner didn't have credits either, but he was a specialist in the field, and this makes a difference. I emphasized that the possibility of selling this pilot was very slim. Selling a series is like winning the lottery.

Two weeks after the series bible went out, we got three offers—Children's Television Workshop, Columbia Studios, and an independent company with a successful show on the air that shall go nameless.

My agent asked me who I wanted to go with, and I said CTW. She said that was crazy; it was the worst offer on the table, and it was. There was no rationale for my thinking that it was the best place to take the project.

The indie company was offering the best money, and my partner and I would be producing; still, I had a bad feeling about it. These people had done nothing to me, so it made no sense.

While nailing down the terms of the contract, they kept asking me about the woman with no credits, how she got "created by," and what exactly she was bringing to the table.

I fought for my assistant, almost to the point of losing the contract. She ended up keeping her "created by" credit, plus having a guarantee to write an episode on the first season, with my overseeing her writing, and two episodes on the second season. This is unheard-of. Writers with no credits don't understand this.

If you've ever seen a Hollywood contract, it covers every fathomable scenario that could possibly happen, even the ridiculous figures that would accrue if your series became the next *Star Wars* trilogy. The numbers on the contract were monopoly money, but legally Hollywood has to cover itself, and wouldn't it be nice if that miracle happened. Jim and I were not only sharing "created by" credit, we were on staff and producing, so our figures were very impressive. For my assistant they were much less impressive. She was certain we were screwing her.

The biggest problem working with nonpros has nothing

to do with their talent but everything to do with their igno-rance of the business. I told her she should be doing head-stands. Series don't sell like this: it is never this easy. But this was her first project. I really believe she thought she was on her way to becoming the next Steven Bochco. To this day she is convinced I was unfair and she hasn't spoken to me.

If new writers ever have the opportunity to ride on a cred-ited writer's coattails, they should take whatever they can get and be grateful for it! It is their way in. They don't know how lucky they are!

Maybe this falling-out with my friend was the reason I got these bad feelings I couldn't explain about this indie company.

And then the Northridge earthquake hit, and the house belonging to the producer who owned the company, and whom we were meeting that day, split in half with the producer in it! The earthquake was emotionally damaging to everybody, but this per-son was severely traumatized. Even the company offices suffered terrible damages. It wasn't very long after that that the producer closed up shop and relocated out of the state to Austin, Texas. And that was the end of *Space Trackers*.

My biggest mistakes in the business have come from not listening to my instinct. It's hard to defend a point of view that doesn't have a lot of logic attached. Now I simply say I've got a very strong feeling about something, and I say it with enough confidence that whomever I am talking to listens. In fact people are pretty open to it. You really don't have to explain it at all. They get it.

A WORD FROM ANIMATION WRITER
STAN BERKOWITZ

Writer Stan Berkowitz holds two daytime Emmy awards for his work on the animated series *The New Batman/Superman Adventures* and *Batman Beyond*. He has held staff positions on *T.J. Hooker*, *Houston Knights*, and *Superboy* and recently completed his first animated feature film, *Justice League, the New Frontier* for video.

MD: You're a graduate of UCLA film school. What is your take on film school for young writers?

SB: I don't think I got that great of an education in film school. I could have gotten the same education by watching movies, reading books, and working in the industry. But you make friends in film school. The people that are most likely to be in the business begin in film school. Industry people send their kids there. That's how you really advance in the business—through friendships.

MD: How did you make the transition from live action to animation?

SB: It was through someone who wrote for *Superboy*. He was a comic book writer mainly, but he was also very good at TV writing. He called me the end of 1993 and said someone he knew was story-editing a Spider Man TV series, and asked if I wanted to do animation. Animation story editors seem to be impressed by writers with live-action credits, and I had a lot of them. I thought I probably could do it.

MD: How do live action and animation differ? I read *Batman* and it seems to have a lot more direction in it than a live-action script. It runs thirty-eight pages.

SB: A half hour of live-action script would run about twenty-eight pages, but in animation, you're calling the shots and describing the action in greater detail, so the scripts run longer.

MD: *Batman* had a teaser and three acts. Does animation format vary like it does with the various episodic TV shows?

SB: Yeah, you might not have a teaser, or you might have a tag. It all depends on the series.

MD: How long did your feature film, *Justice League, the New Frontier*, run?

SB: The running time is about 75 minutes. The script is about 118 pages.

MD: So animation doesn't run a minute per page like live action.

SB: No, it runs faster. Less is happening on camera with animation, so you've got to move faster. You're cutting within the scenes and between the scenes faster. You can't have as many of those great moments where you can show what an actor is thinking. It's much harder to do that in animation.

MD: What's in the future for animation?

SB: It's growing. Computer animation is getting more and more sophisticated; the Writers Guild is already arbitrating arguments over whether something is live action or animated. So in that one sense, at least, I think more things will fall into the technical definition of animation even though they won't look like traditional animation.

MD: So live-action writers and animation writers will all cross over?

SB: There's really no difference. We're storytellers. For example, Paul Dini is a very well known animation writer, yet he got snapped up to be on the staff for the first season of *Lost*. The difference between writing live action and animation is really subtle.

MD: Tell us about your movie.

SB: *The New Frontier* is a very long graphic novel that uses almost all of the DC Comics characters. To adapt it to animation, DC and Warners needed someone who knew what to cut and what to leave in. I discovered the best way was to go to the climax, and if a character wasn't involved in it, I'd go back to the beginning and trim their part. So I learned to work backward. The other thing I learned is, it's better to tell the audience a little too little than a little too much. There's less exposition.

MD: Right, that way the audience gets caught up in the discovery process.

SB: But you've got to pay it off.

MD: I was on a plane coming back from Northern California and found myself sitting next to one of the editors for *The New Frontier*. He said it was terrific. He was right. I waited for its release and really loved it. What's your advice to writers wanting to break into animation?

SB: I'd write spec live-action features. It's the best indi-
cation of the breadth and depth of a writer's creativity. There's also the possibility that a feature script
could serve as more than a writing sample—it could
actually be sold. If your goal is to write episodic animation, it would also be a good idea to write some
sample scripts for the kinds of shows you'd like to
write for.

MD: Daytime animation as opposed to prime-time?

SB: I was talking about daytime shows. The prime-time
broadcast shows like *The Simpsons* are mostly staffed
by established comedy writers. Daytime is a little looser
and the stakes are much smaller: scripts go for five to
seven thousand, so executives are more willing to take
chances on newcomers. As for getting showrunners
to read these samples, you might try meeting them at
comic conventions like the ones in San Diego and San
Francisco. My best advice is to keep writing interesting feature scripts, and don't try to pander. Be yourself.
You still might fail, but at least you'll have done so on
your own terms. Persistence is usually rewarded. In
my case, it took more than eleven years for me to start
making my living as a TV writer.

A WORD FROM REALITY WRITER GARDNER LINN

Gardner Linn was a reality writer on *America's Next Top Model*
and a story producer on the reality show *Black Gold* for TruTV.

He is now the story producer on the new show *Ax Men* for the History Channel.

MD: How did you break into reality writing? What was your background?

GL: Magazine journalism. I decided to move to LA to pursue a screenwriting career. I knew someone who worked on the reality show *Worst-Case Scenario*. They needed a logger.

MD: What do loggers do?

GL: A lot of writers in reality begin as loggers. There's hundreds of hours of footage taken in reality programming. Loggers make the footage searchable.

MD: So it's like data entry?

GL: Basically, except instead of typing in numbers, we'd watch what was happening on screen and enter it in one- and two-minute clips. Like on *America's Next Top Model*, we'd get an hourlong tape of the girls, watch it, and then enter what happens in clips, like "Maggie yells at Lisa . . ." into the database so the writers and editors could search it. That's what I started out doing, also transcribing interviews.

MD: So reality writing has similarities to editing.

GL: It's a combination of writing and editing. We put together moments from the footage and also bites from the interviews to create stories. Every show does it differently. They all have different ways of doing things.

MD: When I first heard the term *reality script*, it sounded like an oxymoron. What exactly is it? Start from the beginning.

GL: *America's Next Top Model* was all very structured before shooting. The executive producer and producers all have specific jobs. They begin by sitting in a room and deciding what the theme for the show will be that week. There's always a lesson on that theme, a challenge, and a photo shoot that relates to the theme—that was the format.

MD: And the writer has nothing to do with this?

GL: That's right. Sometimes we would help brainstorm themes and ideas, but we can usually come in later. The producers decide what the girls will be doing for at least a few hours every day. Then the directors and field directors go out and shoot a lot of footage called *OTFs, on-the-fly interviews*. And once a week they'll usually do sit-down interviews in a studio that cover everything that happened that week. All that footage then comes back to the people in post.

MD: And that's where the writers are.

GL: Yeah, with the editors. We've been in touch with people in the field, so we know what's been going on—who's in trouble, whose story is starting to take shape, if there's been a fight between two girls, things that you can start building out from. We're not really writing anything except the voice-overs. On *Top Model*, we'd put together a script from the interview transcripts and our notes on the scenes, but on my new show we all use Avid Xpress, which is a scaled-down version of the Avid editing software that the editors use. We make a rough cut that's called a *string-out*. Once we get the string-out done, I am usually sitting in the bay with the editor.

MD: So a string-out is a rough cut that you've paired down?

GL: It's a very rough cut that's chunked out and tells a story. Most editors I've worked with have been amazing. It's a real collaboration. They'll take my ideas and insert their own and suggest things I didn't think about. I do the same, and together we come up with something even better. In reality everything has to be about the characters. It's not just about Susie putting on her makeup— it's about why she's doing it. That's what separates the good editors and writers from the bad ones—how they can focus in on the characters and turn ordinary moments into compelling TV.

MD: That's awesome. You're essentially filmmakers. But it sounds pretty technical.

GL: The basic skills you need are not that different from any other kind of writing. Technical skills on the Avid Xpress can be learned in a day or two. It's like learning Final Draft. The editor uses a much more complex system.

MD: What does a reality script look like?

GL: It's anywhere from thirty to fifty pages. It breaks down into five acts per show. The fourth and fifth acts are always the judging and elimination. In the script there are two columns, one for the time code and one for the scene description so the editor can mark it. "1:15, Maggie puts on a dress . . . 1:20, Annie yells to Maggie that's my dress . . ."

MD: Would you recommend that writers interested in reality take some editing classes?

GL: In the future, reality's going more and more toward editing. They are starting to do this thing now called *preda-
tors*, which are producer editors. I think that's where it
is going. Instead of looking for story producers, they'll
be looking for editors who are strong in story. I think
the story producer's job is going to get phased out little
by little.

MD: I get approached all the time by people who say they
have a great idea for a reality show. What would you say
to them?

GL: That happens to me too. Personally I don't know anyone who has sold an idea or gotten it on the air that
hasn't already proven themselves, and even then it's
still tough. I have a friend with a lot of credits. He has
produced and even been a showrunner. He has a great
idea and is working with an authority in the "world"
he's trying to sell, and he's still having trouble.

MD: How's he marketing the show?

GL: He's got it on five or six pages and he's pitching it
around town. But he's got credits. The creator/pro-
ducer of *Black Gold*, who I'm working for now, did a
lot of staff writing on another reality show for the same
company.

MD: So it works like episodic TV. Writers can work up from
a staff position, earn experience and credibility, and
make the contacts so the power people listen.

GL: Yeah, it's not like you can write a spec script. The best
way to break into reality is to either know somebody or
try and get a job in reality, like as a logger, or in some

other capacity and work your way up. If you can type fast, you can be a logger. There's a Web site called RealityStaff.com that a lot of companies use to list job openings. You can also post your resume there. I've never gotten a job off it, but I know people who have. You can be a PA (producer's assistant) or a writer's assistant; those jobs don't require special skills.

14.

SO IT'S WRITTEN: WHAT DO I DO NOW?

I HAVE DISCOVERED THROUGH MY various workshops and speaking engagements that writers are often more interested in marketing their scripts than they are in writing them. "How do you break in?" they'll passionately ask. "Tell me what to do."

At this point, I respond with questions of my own. "Tell me where you're at with your writing. Do you have two series specs in your genre? Are they in different tones and do they show your versatility? What about a polished screenplay or a spec pilot that shows you have an original voice?"

The greatest marketing tools you will ever possess are your completed scripts. All the doors you will ever open lie within the quality of your own writing. It shows on the pages. It must be the best you've got. When you're ready—

The first thing to do is to protect your material. Register it online, or by mail with the Writers Guild (see Appendix A). The WGAW allows members and nonmembers to archive their work for proof of authorship, title credits, and the date it was submitted. The cost to nonmembers is twenty dollars, and the material is registered for six years.

Next, find an agent. Get a list of franchised agents at the Writers Guild of America. They need to be signatories of the Guild; otherwise you don't want them. Make sure you find agents who work in television; some of them don't. It's easy to find out: just make some phone calls, or call the Writers Guild. I'm not going to go into a long explanation on how to choose the right agent, because you'll be lucky to get one. With agents, what's important is that they believe in your material. If they turn out to be awful, they are easy to get rid of. You simply wait a few months, write a nice letter thanking them for their efforts, and say you've decided go elsewhere. Keep records! When you look for another agent, it will be as a formerly represented writer, and it'll be easier.

Agents today want a fast turnover—that is, they will take on a project if they feel they can sell it fast. Many have a large stable of TV writers that they are trying to get on a series staff or get hired to write an episode. It's harder today because of the immense popularity of reality shows.

Eventually, a writer does need an agent, but there are places you can submit to without one if you sign a release form. This essentially releases the producer or readers from liability if they are developing a similar work. Trust me, they are as freaked out about lawsuits as you are. You still can sue, but signing a release makes a lawsuit harder to win.

Yes, writers do get ripped off, but it's not as prevalent as you may think. I hate to say this, but writers are the easiest people in the world to buy off. There's only one alternative to signing a release form, and that's not getting your material read at all. I recommend that if you are asked, go ahead and sign one. Exposure always carries a risk, but it's better than no exposure at all.

While you're waiting for an agent, don't stop writing, and continue marketing. There are other things you can do.

Go to conferences and seminars. Not to sell anything but to meet people in the industry. These are wonderful places to get information, shake hands, take a card, and drop a note later. You get acquainted with companies, the people who buy, and what they're looking for. Check to see if there is a panel of Hollywood agents. If there is, get there early and get a seat up front. If you have the opportunity afterward, go up and introduce yourself. Tell them who you are and what you're doing. Later, when you mention you've made contact with them, it makes a difference.

Do not wait in line all day waiting to pitch your projects in hopes of selling them and miss all these great panels! I've taught pitching at conferences, and I've also been pitched to representing a company. Too many writers put their attention on getting a sale. Their time could be better spent getting information from the pros. Conferences provide access. Learn how to work them; don't let them work you. They aren't cheap, but you can get more done in a few days there then you can in six months on your own. They are especially wonderful for out-of-town writers.

Keep your eyes open for conferences out of the LA area. Sometimes you can even make better contacts at seminars and conferences out of town. They put all the speakers up in the same hotel. At night, everybody goes to the bar. Everybody's loose, they're happy, and they're captive. They have nowhere else to go. It's a terrific way to make connections.

Check out classes and workshops. Kevin Falls heard about a rewriting program at the American Film Institute and submitted one of his scripts there. He was living in Northern California at the time and commuted to LA once a week for the class. The instructor there referred him to an agent.

Explore the Internet. I used to be wary too, but I've found three projects online that we've taken to Lifetime and Hallmark. I got word yesterday that Lifetime was looking for wedding stories. I went to inktip.com, searched under the genres and the subtitle "weddings," and started looking through synopses. Only producers and agents can hit your log line and synopsis. No one else can access the information. If they like what they see, they ask to read your script. Some witers have found great success marketing online.

A few screenwriting contests are impressive (see Appendix B), but there are way too many. I know of one (in a big city) that gives an award to everyone who enters! Be sure to check out the contest thoroughly and who is doing the judging.

Impressive contests provide exposure. The people doing the reading are pros, and they have access into the industry.

A number of years ago I asked my agent if she would like to judge a screenwriting panel. She said a flat "no." I told her the contest was in Hawaii. Then she asked, "How many scripts do I have to read?" I told her the ten finalists.

She still didn't commit, and then I said they put you up for a week at the Hilton Hawaiian Village. She said okay, but she had no intention of taking on any new clients.

On the flight home I discovered that she had signed up a writer. She didn't want new clients, but she had found a project she loved. This is how contests can help you in the back door. The goal is not so much the prize as it is gaining access to industry professionals.

Fellowships are terrific, if you can get one. (See Appendix B.) Two of my former writers won a Disney fellowship, one in features, and one in television. The woman in television was working on staff a year later.

Use creative marketing strategies. Don't think because you wrote "fade out, the end," the creative process ends. Everybody who ever broke into the industry has a different story on how they went about it. Tales of marketing strategies and landing that much-needed break are about as diverse and creative as the writers who tell them.

I learned there was a man in my apartment complex who knew a man who knew another man who played tennis with an agent. I invited him over for dinner and filled him with wine and pasta, then asked him if he would give our script to the man he knew who knew the man who played tennis with the agent. Somehow our script landed at the agent's office. I had a good feeling. In my gut I knew this was it. We were going to be his clients. I waited for the phone call, and I waited, and I waited. The call never came. Finally, I called him. I was scared to death, as I introduced myself as the writer whose material had been referred to him. He barely remembered the script. The dialogue went something like this:

```
INTERCUT TELEPHONE CONVERSATION:


                    AGENT
          Yeah . . . oh, right. The script had
          some good stuff in it. Keep writing.
          You got some talent.

                    MYSELF
          Thank you . . .
A long, uncomfortable pause. I was waiting for him to
say more.

                    MYSELF
          We're looking for representation and
          we thought—

                    AGENT
               (cutting me off)
          I'm not looking for new clients.

                    MYSELF
          Oh . . . well ah, do you think we
          could come in and meet you?

                    AGENT
          Why do you want to meet me? I'm not
          taking on new clients.

                    MYSELF
          We really appreciate your reading our
          script. It'll only take a minute. We
          just want to shake your hand.
```

And so began my twenty-five years of creative lying. We met the agent and the meeting was indeed short. He still had no intention of signing us, but we did have a great rapport. I think, quite honestly, he got a kick out of us. We were aggressive but not obnoxious, overly enthusiastic, young, and hopeful. Before we left, I asked him for just one more favor. Though he had no intention of handling us, would he please just submit the script on our behalf, just so somebody—anybody—would read it. At this point, I think all he wanted was to get us out of his office, and so he agreed. The agent a year later signed us on. For almost twenty-three years (a few I strayed) he worked as my agent. And in all that time his telephone personality has never changed.

Everybody who ever succeeded in this industry has a different story on how it happened for them. No matter how you proceed, eventually you have to find an agent. There is a remote chance you could sell a script without an agent. It is impossible, however, to have a career without one. Agents are crucial.

A WORD FROM AGENT MITCHEL STEIN

Mitchel Stein, talent and literary representative for the Stein Agency.

MD: Why does a writer need an agent?

MS: You're not considered real in this town without having representation. It means your material is of high caliber. In order to submit to the studios, your work needs to come through an agent. But it's a catch-22: agents don't want to represent you unless you're currently represented or have had something produced. And it's difficult to be produced unless you have representation.

MD: Yet many new writers do find representation.

MS: True. Every year agencies take a handful of new writers.

MD: How do these writers get read?

MS: Almost always, without exception, it's through a personal contact. An attorney might call who I worked with five years ago and say he has a friend who wrote a script. Will I take a look at it? Or a studio exec might say he found a writer who he thinks is a genius. I'll ask if he or she has representation. He might say, "Yes, but he's not happy with them." As quickly as I read material, I find that I still have stacks of scripts being shuffled around. There is very little surface in my house that doesn't have a script that needs to be read.

MD: What does a writer need to break into television?

MS: It's important to have a couple of spec samples in the genre you choose—half hour or hour. It's also good to have an original spec pilot or a feature. One shows that you can "parrot," i.e., mirror or mimic, and the other shows you have a voice. The sample specs should have different tones. It shows you can write for a variety of shows.

MD: You're primarily a TV agency, but do you read features?

MS: I read them, but not necessarily to sell. I'm not in the script business. I'm in the business of looking for writers who have talent that can grow with me. I want to read their best samples. If I find something that excites me, I'll call them up and ask what else they have.

A young man I'm starting to work with wrote a spec *Wire*. I've watched the show enough to get an idea of it, but I don't know it that well. Often, I will tell writers to give me a short paragraph up front on the show at the beginning of the script on a page of its own. This guy did something very clever: he wrote, "Previously on *The Wire* . . ." It was economic, and it brought me up to what I needed, no more. There were no detailed breakdowns. He gave me the setting and who the characters were and that's all I wanted to know. That's all I need, five sentences, and I can get into the script.

MD: What do you consider a good read?

MS: I like clever dialogue, interesting characters, and sound structure. I also like to see a lot of white on the pages. One thing that turns me off is when I open up the script and there is page after page of single-spaced detailed descriptions and camera angles. Don't tell me how I'm supposed to visualize, and don't tell the director how to do his job. It's just extra clutter.

I'm a minimalist. I hate exposition. If I see it on the first page of a script, I won't read it. Don't explain things to me. Let me figure them out.

Typos make me crazy. If I get a typo on the first page, I'm done. If you don't care enough about a glaring mistake, then I'm not going to deal with it. Don't tell me it's all about the art. If you want art, be a poet. I don't like sloppy work.

MD: What about television movies?

MS: Long form is dead. NBC and CBS have pretty much shut down.

MD: There's cable movies.

MS: If you're talking about the Hallmark Channel or Lifetime and you've got a small movie that can be made for a million and that fits what they are looking for, it is very easy to get it submitted. But the terms are bad. Nobody wants to work with them because they just don't pay enough money.

MD: What about HBO and Showtime?

MS: They want George Clooney's and Tom Hanks's company. They have become very elitist and star-driven. It didn't used to be that way.

MD: Do you represent animation writers?

MS: I'd say quite a few, relative to the size of my agency. I represent a young man who had a bunch of specs, everything from *My Name Is Earl* to *The Office*. I submitted them to Disney, and they responded well. He's now doing animation for them. I also represent two great comic writers who used to write for the Johnny Carson show. Their humor is hysterical—caustic, very acerbic, and yet they write to an eight-year-old marketplace. I got a call from Australia yesterday; they want them to write the opening episodes for a series. These writers are very bright. They don't talk down to an eight-year-old audience. It's really interesting, you don't need an animation spec sample to break in. A good half-hour comedy spec will do.

MD: You're talking about daytime animation?

MS: Yeah, I'm talking about kids.

MD: What about action animation, like for *Batman*?

MS: Then you need an action spec script in that genre.

MD: What are your thoughts on screenwriting competitions?

MS: To me, they mean very little. There are a couple where I might read the winner, like the AFI or the Nicholls. Then again, there are baby agents who are just starting out and they are happy to read anything they can get their hands on. They inundate themselves with hundreds and hundreds of scripts because they are so eager to find the acorn. Over the years, for every hundred unsolicited scripts I've read, as many as one has ever panned out.

MD: What about the new Internet market techniques?

MS: Here is the problem, it's the future, but I don't think anybody's ready for it yet. Let's face it, everybody goes to these symposiums, where experts talk about how we're going to monetize the future. How are we going to monetize the Web? How are we we going to monetize mobisodes, and you know what? They haven't figured it out, either. So we all go play in it and get our toes wet so when things start to happen, we can say we had the experience and that we all flailed around in it together.

MD: What do you think of the Christian market?

MS: I think there is a huge market for it, but there's no money there right now. In the end the faith-based networks just don't have any money to spend.

MD: What's the difference between a writer being persistent and a writer being a pain? What do you expect from your clients?

MS: I think it's imperative that the writer know how to push the agent's buttons. You have to know the fine line between motivating your agent and turning him off. Some people who call me once a month are a pain in the ass. Some people who call me twice a day are being persistent. It depends on the personality, the relationship. People skills are as important as writing in this business.

MD: Do clients have to do their own marketing?

MS: No, but it sure helps. Agents have many clients; the writer has only one. Some writers sit home and never call and wait for the phone to ring. Others call up saying they've just spoken to a producer and to please send a script over to them. We hope that that writer will be out there as much as we are.

MD: Any words of wisdom to end on?

MS: If you really want to know about the business ask somebody who has been in it for six months.

MD: And on that, we both have to laugh.

15.

THE MOST FREQUENTLY ASKED QUESTIONS ABOUT MARKETING

How do I get an agent?

A referral from an industry insider is the best way. A writer or producer preferably, because they read scripts. If you don't know a Hollywood insider, go to a conference and meet one. Contacts can be made.

How are agents paid?

All franchised agents receive 10 percent of what the writer earns. These are agents who have subscribed to the Writers Guild of America Artists Managers Basic Agreement. They deal with studios and producers who are signatories of the Guild. Only look for a franchised agent.

Do agents have reader fees?

Franchised agents cannot charge for reading scripts. They are looking at your material as a possible source of income for themselves and, therefore, have a personal interest at stake.

How do I find a list of franchised agents?

A list can be easily acquired by contacting the Writers Guild of America: http://www.wga.org/agency/agencylist.asp#op.

Do agents critique your work?

Rarely. Their interest is in whether or not they can market your material—not where the material went wrong. Don't look for a detailed analysis from an agent.

Which is better: to sign with a small agency or a large agency?

Don't worry about whether the agency is small or large. What matters is the agent's belief in you as a writer. It is most likely in the beginning that you will end up at a smaller agency. This can be an advantage, since with the larger agencies, it is easier to get lost in the shuffle.

Does an agent keep me informed?

Yes. The writer should be made aware of each and every submission. If the agent does not offer this information, it is up to you to stay on top of the situation. Don't be a nuisance, but do check in periodically and find out what's going on. E-mail is useful this way.

What if I already have a literary agent?

If this agent does not handle film, then ask for a referral. Many literary agents have agreements with film agents, and they receive a finder's fee. A reference from a professional works wonders in getting your material read.

Can I use more than one film agent?

Once you make an agreement with an agent, you can only use that particular agent to represent your material.

Are there agents who handle both film and publishing?

Yes. If you are interested in working in both mediums, it might be advantageous for you to find an agent who deals with both. You can find these agents by looking them up in *Writer's Market* and other resource books.

What is an option?

An option is a fee that is paid by the studio or producer for movie or television rights to your script. In return, the writer promises not to shop the script anywhere else until the option period has expired.

Today, free options are becoming more and more common. Some indie producers and smaller companies don't have the money but believe in the project and are willing to put in the time. Last year I signed three option agreements. The average option runs a year. If, during this time, the studio or production company decides to make the film, they package, develop, bring the finances together, and do everything needed to get the movie into production.

Can I submit my scripts to production companies without the help of an agent?

Yes. But first you must identify these production companies, where they are, and how to reach them. A book I find very helpful for this is the *Hollywood Creative Directory*. This handy publication comes out quarterly and lists hundreds of independent producers, their addresses, and phone numbers. Many independent production companies will read unsolicited material.

Once my script is submitted, who will most likely read it?

Many production companies, as well as the larger agencies, have a screening process. That process begins in almost every instance with a *reader* or *story analyst*. Their job is to supply *coverage* for the higher-ups. Coverage consists of the property title, who wrote it, the type of material it is, the length, and certain elements, if any, that stand out. In addition, a TV guideline, or a two-sentence log line is included and whether the reader recommends the material or gives it a pass. It's attached with a two-page synopsis of the script.

Can I begin the marketing process before my script is complete?

Gain knowledge about the industry. Start preparing a marketing strategy. Read the industry trades and journals, go to conferences, and start accumulating names of possible contacts. Don't attempt to start marketing a script before you are finished writing it. If someone wants to see your material and it's not ready, you could lose the contact and their interest by the time it is.

Exactly what are the trades?

The *trades*, as they are referred to by the industry, are the *Daily Variety* and the *Hollywood Reporter*. Both journals are delivered five working days a week. Everything a writer needs to know is listed here—from Hollywood gossip and finances to what is in production, who is doing it, and where. Even productions scheduled for the future are listed. Since both journals cover the same information, it is only necessary to order one.

I hear the word turnaround a lot. What exactly does that mean?

Turnaround happens when a company owns a script or other property, but the contract says that after a certain amount of time the material reverts back to the writer. At that point the writer can take it out again to another company. Many movies get purchased in turnaround.

Is it true you need contacts to break into the industry?

There is no denying that contacts are a crucial part of breaking in. The good news is, contacts can be made at writer's conferences, contests, and workshops. Your uncle does not have to own a studio.

Can I sell an idea?

It's very tough these days. Producers and companies want spec scripts; they don't want treatments and synopses. There are exceptions to this, but they're rare. Robert Kosberg, who is considered the king of pitch, looks at ideas and, if they are hot, will pitch them for you. Go to his site at http://www.moviepitch.com/.

When I submit the script, should I include a synopsis of the story?

No. This encourages readers not to read. You only need to submit a synopsis when one is requested. In the event that it is asked for, the writing must be tight (no more than one page) and should entice the reader to dive into the script.

Before submitting material to agents or production companies, should I send a query letter?

I tell writers not to send in scripts but to send query letters instead. Query letters need to grab readers so they say, "Yes, I want to take a look at this." Briefly introduce yourself, then go to work selling confidence in your material. Always try to come from a place of strength. If you've made previous contact with the individual, mention it. Nobody cares about how many degrees or children you have. But if you are an authority on the topic you choose to write about, mention that (i.e., a police officer who has written a crime story, or a physician who has scripted a medical mystery).

If your script is high-concept, give the log line. If it isn't, point out the strengths in the material. Is it a star vehicle (does it have powerful roles for a male or female lead)? Is it a fresh idea? Is it timely? Will it reach a mass audience? Find words that will pique interest in your material. Mention you will be contacting them with a follow-up phone call or e-mail. This leaves the ball in your hands. Wait three weeks and call or e-mail them. They probably won't have read it by then, but continue to contact them every few weeks until they do. Get to know the secretary's name, and ask for him or her. Secretaries are some of the most powerful people in the business. They can provide you with valuable information.

Do I need to send a self-addressed stamped envelope with my material?

I highly recommend that you don't send the script unless it is asked for. People get mad when they have to send back material on their dime, or even on your dime because they have to take the time.

Do I submit my script to the production company, or to an individual who works for that company?

Never submit your script to a company. It will surely get lost in the mail room. You need to get names out of the *Hollywood Creative Directory* or use the phone and get a name. This way, your script lands on someone's desk. At that point, it may be referred to a reader. The trades will also mention individuals who work for production companies.

If an independent producer or company is interested in making a deal and I don't have an agent, what should I do?

This is the ideal time for you to find an agent. Ask the producers you are working with if they can recommend someone. This is a great way to get into a good agency. If that doesn't work, you can use the serious interest to open doors and find somebody to rep you. Don't be greedy and say, "Why should I give up ten percent of my fee when I'm the one who got the job?" Never try to negotiate your own deal.

A good agent is well worth 10 percent when it comes to finding loopholes. Remember, agents want what's best for you because it means more for them as well. The only viable alternative is an entertainment attorney. Be wary of their fees. You may not be saving money in the long run.

How much well I get paid?

A full list of scale payments can be found by going to wga.org or contacting the WGA contract department at 323-782-4501 and asking for the book on minimum wage agreements.

Do episodic television shows have readers?

No, this job belongs to the story editor. Many agents have readers, and baby agents (new agents) are sometimes eager to read to find new clients. It is much more difficult to get a spec television script read than a two-hour movie script read. Most television shows will not read unsolicited material. It is crucial, therefore, to write a few spec scripts for various existing shows and, on their merit, find an agent who will go to bat for you.

How can I get my spec script to a company?

The best way is through an agent or a personal connection. Companies won't read unsolicited scripts. If you can't do this, then make a personal connection. Go to seminars and places where you can meet showrunners and talk to people in television. Follow up those meetings with a note or a telephone call. Connections can be made.

How does a writer submit a pilot?

Write the spec pilot as a sample to show your originality, not with the intention of selling it. You should back this up with a couple of other specs to prove you can write for existing shows. Agents will like this. It will show your voice and your versatility. Networks buy names, not ideas. They want writers with track records.

How much money does a spec screenplay sell for?

It can go for as low as $30,000 for a movie budgeted at under $2 million, and as high as six figures, but that is exceptionally rare and only happens if you are an A-list writer or you get caught up in a bidding war (that's when two companies want your script and keep pushing the price up). I don't know about you, but this kind of war I totally support. I would take no sides and "mission accomplished." But if your sole purpose is to make money, there are easier ways to do it—like take out a loan, go to Las Vegas, and put your money on red. You have much better odds at roulette.

Can I mail in only a portion of my script to interest the reader?

Only do this when you are asked to. There are some agents who request only the first ten pages of your script, but this is rare. Never attempt to submit the first ten pages unless your script is complete. In the event that a reader or agent requests the rest of the material, be very certain you have it.

Should I get a professional critique, and how do I choose a script consultant?

This is a very good question. Yes. It is very important that you receive an in-depth critique before submission. Writers become too close to their material, and they need an outside opinion. Also, a good consultant can help take your material to a professional level. And if they feel your material sings they can refer you to an agent. In an industry as competitive as this one, you definitely need an edge.

Consultants can be found on many sites and in scriptwriting magazines. Be sure that when you contact these people, you understand what you are getting for your money. You don't want coverage, which is a synopsis of the story, a grade for your writing, and somebody telling you what doesn't work. You need a writer or professional who has been there and done it, and who knows how to get inside the material and fix it. That's what I do, and many of my associates, some of whom I highly respect. Coverage is a different matter, and you're going to get that anyway. Get your material right first.

There are some script consultants who are excellent, and some who should try another line of work. Some are pricey; some you need to take out a second mortgage on your home for! Beware of anyone who promises you anything other than good work.

Is it a disadvantage to try to work and sell while living away from the Los Angeles area?

For those in episodic television, living in the area is a must because there are so many meetings. In features and TV movies, it's sometime done, but commuting gets expensive. The good news is, you can write specs anywhere. I know some very successful writers who feel the sacrifices are worth it. For now, don't worry about where you live. Worry about the quality of your material. After you get a sale, then make a choice.

If I sell my script, can I be guaranteed the movie or television show will get made?

No. Just because a sale takes place and money changes hands, there is no guarantee the television show or film will get made. Often the reasons have nothing to do with the quality of the material. Don't fret: you have a legitimate credit anyway. You'll get paid, and it will pave the way to another job. It's disappointing, but at least you'll have made a hefty deposit.

If I made a low-budget film or demo short, would my chances be better at getting an agent than if I write a spec script?

If what you have is good, it can open doors, especially if you're interested in becoming a writer/director. There are many people in the industry who would rather watch a movie or short than read a script. The relevant word here is *good*. How good? And beware of the cost incurred. And it would be even sweeter accompanied by a script.

What if I disagree with the notes my agent and producers give me?

This could be a problem. The agent has to believe in your material in order to sell it. You better be very sure it's not your ego and stubbornness getting in the way. Many times I've been given notes I didn't like, and I was able to adjust the material and tweak it in ways that made us both happy. Often agents and producers know something's not working but are unable to identify what it is or how to fix it. So writers have to interpret. Find the best way you can to deal with their notes. Discuss, negotiate, suggest, and ask "what if?" Do whatever you can if you plan on getting invited back.

Once my script is complete, should I spend the majority of my time marketing, or should I begin another project?

Begin another project. Under all circumstances, you must continue to write, but market your script while you are writing. A well-written script is an excellent calling card, but it's often not enough. If they like what you have, production companies will want to see more.

How can I become a member of the Writers Guild?

The guild works on a point system based on writing employment with a "signatory" company (a company that has signed the Guild's collective bargaining agreement). You must earn twenty-four credits for full membership in the three years preceding application, and there is an associate membership for writers with less credit, who meet other specifications. Since the WGA West and the WGA East have different rules, I would go online or contact the Guild you will be joining for details. For WGAW, contact wga.org or call the membership department at 323-782-4532. Contact WGAE at wgaeast.org or call 212-767-7800.

16.

A FINAL NOTE FROM THE AUTHOR

ONE MORNING THERE WAS A knock at my door. I stood there with a cup of coffee in my hand and no makeup on while a very distraught student paced back and forth telling me she could no longer continue in my workshop. Her therapist told her she needed to confront me. She was stuck on her script, writing was too hard, and she wanted out. I had no idea the workshop was causing this woman such pain. Writing can be challenging, but it shouldn't be waterboarding! I certainly understood if she wanted to quit.

A month later when she showed up in class, I was very surprised. When she passed around her work to the seven other writers, we were all blown away. Her writing had taken a giant leap. In fact, her script later made it into the quarterfinals of the Nicholl Fellowship.

As writers, it is our job to place obstacles in the pathway of our protagonists. Obstacles create the necessary conflict that forces our characters to take action. It's not what they get, it's what they don't get that moves the story forward. As with our characters, the obstacles we face as writers can push us to triumph. In my student's case, she had hit a creative wall. Sometimes these walls are there for a purpose. She could have retreated. Instead she scaled it.

I think the same holds true in marketing. As writers, we will all experience rejection. If we step back and see this rejection as a necessary step on the path to our goals, it can serve us. The roadblock forces us to take an alternate route, and that sometimes is the only way we can get there.

For most writers, marketing ourselves is the toughest aspect of our work. Life would be so much easier if we could just hide behind our laptops and write. I tell students that marketing is like standing at the edge of the pool on a very hot day: the pool isn't heated, but you know if you could just let go, after the initial shock you'd be glad you did. If you stand there and overthink it, if you focus on the discomfort instead of the end result, then you'll forgo the experience altogether and never know where it might have led. Mental conditioning is half of everything in this business.

When I look back over my years in the industry, the high points of my career happened when I was in a good mental place, and the low points came when I wasn't. I remember once being cut off from an episode because I delivered a draft an executive producer didn't like. This happens sometimes. I went out that day, bought new curtains for my house, and the next week went on to another job. Years later, when I was going through some difficult times, I got bad coverage on a spec script and was so devastated that I didn't write again for a year. I was the same writer, the quality of my work was good, and so was the script. Coverage is purely subjective. I knew this deep down, but somewhere what had changed was my perception of myself.

If you're serious about pursuing a career in television or film, it is important for you to find a way to detach yourself from your material. Run, meditate, say affirmations or stand on your head. Find whatever it is that works for you and keeps you going. That way, when rejection comes, the disappointment won't deter you from your goals. In effect, you're under the wave instead of letting it hit you in the gut and throw you on the shore.

Also remember, the most important part of writing is the process, not the sale. Of all the writers I have met who haven't sold, none of them have regretted writing the script. Some have healed themselves in the creative process. Others have found great joy in it. They get caught up in the challenge, and they complete their projects, which is an incredible satisfaction in itself.

I wish you happiness and good fortune in your writing.

GLOSSARY

A, B, C, D, E story: Parallel plotlines in an episode in order of their importance.

act: A unit of action in episodic TV that builds to a commercial break. In some cable TV and in all feature films, acts exist but are not noted in script format.

act break: The climactic act end before a commercial, often called a *cliffhanger*.

action/narrative: All the description below the slug line. It tells you everything that is happening on the screen.

arc: How a character changes. Who characters are when the movie begins, the crisis that happens to them, and how they are changed in the end.

baby agent: A new agent who is just starting out. Baby agents usually have trained with or been assistants to an experienced agent, and now they are taking on clients and projects of their own.

baby writer: A writer without a lot of experience who is new on staff.

back life of the character: Everything of consequence that has taken place in the character's life before the story begins.

backstory: The history of a character or story before the episode or movie begins.

beat: 1. A unit or step of the story. 2. A pause in the delivery of dialogue.

beat sheet: A list of story beats, or scenes, sometimes very detailed, sometimes in sequences and more general.

bible: A guide that tells you everything you need to know about a series—the franchise, character biographies, tone of the show, locales, rules of the world, and guidelines for episodes. Bibles that are created for existing series list past episodes and give guidelines to help writers better understand the show. Bibles are also written to set up a series so that buyers can see the overall vision. They list ideas for possible episodes.

breaking a story: Identifying major turning points and act ends in a story.

button: A punch in dialogue or in a scene that helps the cut.

central conflict: The core conflict or problem that confronts the main character or characters and drives the story toward the resolution.

character-driven: Having action coming from the main character so that the character, not the plot, drives the action.

cliffhanger: It used to be the most important act end in an episode. Today, it's used to describe any good act end or season finale.

closure: Completion of a storyline at each episode's end. *House* is a series with closure.

cold opening: The same as a teaser: a unit of action that runs before the show's titles.

compelling characteristic: The driving force in a character. The characteristic that is most dominant.

confrontation: The largest unit of action in the three-act structure, around fifty pages, where the protagonist meets the majority of his obstacles.

core cast: The continuing cast on a series who are in every episode.

dramatic need: What consciously or unconsciously drives the protagonist. Not getting what he or she needs creates the next action.

dramedy: Comedy-drama. The catchphrase came into vogue in the late 1980s to describe the new genre of shows like *The Days and Nights of Molly Dodd* by creator Jay Tarses. The term is rarely used anymore, since comic dramas have become a staple of TV entertainment. An example would be a show like *Weeds*.

dovetail: When two stories come together in the end, they dovetail.

episodic: 1. Describes a unit of script which does not connect or impact another unit of script. A screenplay can be too episodic. 2. A TV show that is the opposite of a serial. Each week it has closure.

exposition: The needed information that must come out for the audience to understand a story.

EXT. The abbreviation for *exterior*, used in screenplay and teleplay slug lines.

first draft: 1. Exactly what it says it is. 2. For the writer, it can be many drafts before he or she lets anybody see them. 3. In development, it's a step, with payment, submitted by the writer before he or she receives the producer's notes.

format: 1. The printed style of a script or teleplay. 2. The structure for a show or a pilot.

franchise: The central core a series is built on. The franchise brings the show and its characters together. *Grey's Anatomy* is a medical franchise centered on the personal and professional lives of interns and their supervisors. Successful movies and series are also franchised. *The Sarah Connor Chronicles* is the first TV show incarnation of the *Terminator* franchise.

freelancer: A writer who is hired independently on a per script basis.

green light: The approval for a script or show to go into production.

high concept: An idea with a very strong hook and broad audience appeal that can be described in one simple sentence.

hook: Anything that grabs an audience in the opening of a TV show or movie. The term *hook*, like *cliffhanger*, is used more broadly today to describe a great twist or any device that grips an audience anywhere in the script.

inferior position: The audience's position when it makes its discoveries with the main characters, not before them. *House*, *Cold Case*, and the *CSI* franchise are all examples. Opposite to the *superior* *position* (*Columbo*), where the audience knows more than the main characters.

INT.: The abbreviation for *interior*, used in slug lines.

legs: When a series has legs, it's got ongoing potential. The characters and arena provide endless storylines. *Friends* had legs.

log line: 1. A one-sentence storyline that could fit into *TV Guide*. 2. A one-or two-sentence description that includes the premise and arc of a storyline.

M.O.: modus operandi, a person's characteristic behavior patterns in committing a crime.

on the nose: Dialogue that is too obvious and not natural.

personal involvement: The personal stake that the main character of the series has in the story. Example: On *Grey's Anatomy*, Dr. Bailey realizes it's her son being rushed into the ER.

plot hole: When there is a logic bomb or flaw in a story.

pointing an arrow: Instead of ignoring a plot flaw, deliberately pointing a finger at it, addressing it, and thereby eradicating the problem.

polish: A finishing touch on a teleplay or screenplay after the rewriting is done.

P.O.V.: Point of view. 1. A story is told from a P.O.V. In *Desperate Housewives*, it is the dead housewife on Wisteria Lane. She gives the voice-over (V.O.) each week. On *Grey's Anatomy*, it is Meredith. Shows do not need V.O.'s to establish a P.O.V. In *Women's Murder Club*, the P.O.V. is always from the perspective of Inspector Lindsay Boxer 2. P.O.V. is an angle as seen through the lens of a camera. It often establishes where a character is looking, i.e., the character's P.O.V.

premise pilot: A pilot episode that introduces the characters and shows the situation that brought them together. An example would be *Lost*. The pilot episode opened on the crashed passenger airliner on the beach.

procedurals: Investigation-based, clue-driven shows that solve a mystery and have closure each week. *House*, *CSI*, and *Women's Murder Club* are examples.

producer: Most producers in episodic television are writers who have moved up the ranks on staff shows, gaining experience and earning credits. TV producers have many titles: executive producer, co-executive producer, supervising producer, and associate producer. The line producer is on the set and in charge of the production.

protagonist: The hero and rooting interest in the story who moves the action forward.

raising the stakes: Compounding conflict for the protagonist so that he or she has much more to lose.

resolution: The last act in the classic three-act structure that builds toward the climax. Protagonists either achieve or do not achieve what they're after.

rewrite: There are many levels of rewrites. Major rewrites can include changing significant story elements, restructuring, adding and/or removing characters, and replacing scenes.

runner: A recurring bit of action or a joke that is not big enough to constitute a C or D story. The magic number of times to play out a runner is three.

scene: A unit of action that is a place (locale) and a time (day or night).

second draft: A draft written after the writer has received notes from a producer.

segue: 1. The transition from one scene to another. 2. In dialogue, the transition from one subject to another.

sequence: A series of important scenes tied together by an overriding singular purpose. Example: the wedding in *The Godfather*.

serial: A series with continuing plotlines that develops over time. *Grey's Anatomy*, *Nip/Tuck*, *Dexter*, *Brothers and Sisters*, and *Weeds* are examples of serials.

setup: The opening that establishes what the story is about. Half-hour shows, one-hour shows, and two-hour movies all have setups.

shooting script: The draft of a script that goes into production.

showrunner: The top dog/executive producer in charge of a series. Showrunners determine every aspect of the show and answer only to the network.

single-camera: A show shot with one camera, and not before a live audience. Usually refers to comedy.

sitcom: A half-hour comedy, either one-camera or three-camera, that tries to hit three laughs a page through character, pacing, and timing.

soap: A serial drama, not restricted to daytime, which is character-driven and has continuing storylines.

soft concept: Unlike a high concept, the soft concept is an idea that lacks the *chink, chink* of big box office. Many Academy Award–nominated movies for Best Screenplay and Best Picture are soft concepts, but soft concepts are a hard sell.

spec pilot: An episode of a new series created by the spec writer as a sample of his or her voice and creativity or in hopes of a sale.

spec script: A speculation script written in hopes of a sale or as a sample to open doors to an eventual sale.

springboard: The idea that everything "springs" from.

staff writer: The first rung of the writing staff. They are sometimes called *baby writers.*

standing sets: The show's sets that remain on stage. Writing an episode that utilizes only those, with no need for swing sets (sets that have to be reset), is called writing an "in-house show." Producers will love you for it, because it's cheap and fast.

step deal: A writer's contract with guaranteed payments and the possibility of *cutoffs* after each draft delivery. If the producer is not satisfied with the writer's work, the writer can be cut off.

story editor: Works above the staff writers and below the producer on a series.

tag: The scene or short scenes that come after the last commercial break. They can wrap up a show or leave a cliffhanger to tease the audience.

teaser: Also called a *cold opening*. The scenes that happen before the
main titles that tease the audience to stay tuned. They can provide
a hook and lead in to that week's story, but don't always.

telegraphing: Writers telling the audience where they are going before
they need to. They are giving away their story.

teleplay: A script written for television.

three-camera series: A comedy shot before a live audience with three
cameras shooting simultaneously.

tone: The mood in a series or screenplay created first by the writer's
vision and expanded from there.

tracking: Tracking a storyline means carefully making sure the time-
line and plot elements all work.

trades: Professional journals of the industry that cover the daily
news.

treatment: A written narrative of the story. Some treatments are short,
some are long, and they vary according to shows. If you are ever
asked to write a treatment, always ask for an example of what is
wanted.

**Writers Guild of America, West, and Writers Guild of America,
East (WGAW and WGAE):** The two branches of the professional union that represents screenwriters.

APPENDIX A

RESOURCES

To Find Scripts

Writers Guild of America, West
7000 West Third Street
Los Angeles, CA 90048
(323) 951-4000
www.wga.org
Has a library open to the public. Open Monday through Friday, 11
a.m. to 5 p.m., and on Thursdays until 8 p.m. Closed the last Friday
of every month.

Writers Guild of America, East
555 West 57th Street
New York, NY 10019
(212) 767-7800
WGA East does not have a script library.

American Film Institute, Louis B. Mayer Library (AFI)
2021 N. Western Avenue
Los Angeles, CA 90027
(323) 856-7654
www.afi.com/about/lubtary.aspx
Published and unpublished screenplays and books on film.

Open Monday through Thursday, 9 a.m. to 5 p.m., and Fridays 9 a.m. to 6 p.m. Saturdays and Sundays, 10 a.m. to 6 p.m.

University of California, Los Angeles (UCLA)
Arts Library of Special Collection
Young Research Library
405 Hilgard Avenue
Los Angeles, CA 90024
By appointment only: (310) 825-7253
www.library.ucla.edu/libraries/arts/speccoll.htm
Call and ask for material ahead of time. They need one or two days' notice. If they do not have what you're looking for, possibly they can refer you to places that might.

University of Southern California (USC)
Cinema-Television Library
Doheny Library
University Park
Los Angeles, CA 90089-0182
(213) 740-3994
www.USC.edu/isd/libraries/locations/cinema_tv/

The best way to locate material in your area is to check out film schools and universities with film departments. Call up their libraries and find out if they have scripts available and if they are open to the public.

To Buy Scripts

Script City
www.scriptcity.com/
Has a great selection of screenplays and teleplays. You can have them sent to you the day of purchase as PDF downloads. The teleplays run $10 each. Screenplays can vary. Often they run specials, or if you buy three screenplays at a time, you get a discount.

Drew's Script-o-Rama
www.script-o-rama.com/
They have a good selection of free screenplays and some teleplays.

Simply Scripts
www.simplyscripts.com/
Also a good selection of free screenplays and some teleplays.

Twiz TV
www.Twiztv.com/
Free teleplays. Many of them not current.

It is important when you are ordering or downloading teleplays or screenplays that you make sure you're getting the actual production scripts, not the transcripts. There are many sites and they are constantly changing. Go to Google and type in movie and television scripts and have fun.

For Networking

The Scriptwriters Network
6404 Wilshire Boulevard #1640
Los Angeles, CA 90048
1-888-SWN-WORD
(1-888-796-9673)
info@ScriptwritersNetwork.org
A nonprofit organization for speaker events, networking, and resources.

For Links and Information

Check out the Open Directory for Writers Resources and the various listings that interest you. There is a lot of free information. Go to television at: http://www.dmoz.org/

Screenwriting Software

Helps television writers and screenwriters format their scripts according to Hollywood standards. The format is very tedious, and the programs save time and energy. They are not difficult to learn, and come in both PC and Mac versions. I highly recommend them to all writers. They are well worth the money.

I have used Final Draft for years and have never experimented with another program, since it has worked so well for me. I learned it in a day or two. I'm dyslexic, so if I can work with it any person can. Most of the people I have worked with in the industry use the Final Draft program. I have also heard good reports on Movie Magic Screenwriter.

Final Draft
http://www.finaldraft.com

Movie Magic Screenwriter
http://www.screenplay.com/

APPENDIX B

FELLOWSHIPS AND WRITING COMPETITIONS

The Nicholl Fellowship
1313 N. Vine Street
Hollywood, CA 90028-8107
www.Oscars.org/nicholl/index.html
Entry fee: $30
Deadline: May 30
The Nicholl is the most prestigious of all the competitions. There are about four thousand submissions a year, and only five fellowships awarded. If you are selected, you will receive $30,000 and be expected to complete a feature film in the fellowship year.

Walt Disney Fellowship Program
Walt Disney Studios & ABC Entertainment
500 S. Buena Vista Street
Burbank, CA 91251-1735
(818) 560-6894
http://www.abctalentdevelopment.com/html/writing_fellowship_mainpage.htm
Entry fee: none
Disney selects up to eight writers to work full time in developing their craft at the Walt Disney Studios and ABC Entertainment. They offer fellowships in feature film and television. No previous experience is necessary. Writing submissions are necessary. The application period is May 1 through June 23.

Nickelodeon Writing Fellowship
Attn: Karen Kirkland
231 West Olive Avenue
Burbank, CA 91502
(818) 736-3663
info.writing@nick.com
Entry fee: none
Nickelodeon offers fellowships in animation as well as live-action TV to culturally and ethnically diverse writers. Provides a paid training phase. Check the Internet for the next cycle of submissions.

Fox Searchlab–Fox Searchlight Pictures
Attn: Susan O' Leary
10201 W. Pico Boulevard
Building 667, Suite #5
Los Angeles, CA 90035
(310) 369-5423
www.foxsearchlight.com/lab/about/index.html
No entry fee and no deadlines
They are currently updating their Web site. Check it for new information.

Sundance Screenwriters' Lab
Sundance Institute
225 Santa Monica Boulevard, 8th Floor
Santa Monica, CA 90401
(310) 394-4662
www.sundance.org
Application fee: $30
Deadline: May 1
Their Feature Film Program includes the January Screenwriters' Lab, the June Filmmakers' Lab, and the June Screenwriters' Lab. There is one application for the Feature Film Program. With this application you will

be considered for all of the programs. The first five pages of your script are required with a synopsis, along with a cover letter and resume.

Zoetrope Screenplay Contest
916 Kearny Street
San Francisco, CA 94133
(415) 788-7500 (telephone); (415) 989-7910 (fax)
http://www.zoetrope.com/contests/
Entry fee: $40 (early entry fee: $30)
The winner and top-ten finalists will be considered for representation by ICM, UTA, and the Paradigm Agency, among others. Their scripts will be considered for film option and development by leading production companies, including American Zoetrope. The early deadline is August 1, and the final deadline September 2.

The competitions are endless, so discriminate! Don't go bankrupt entering all of them. One of the smaller contests I have a special connection to is Monterey County Screenwriting Competition. The judges for the final selections are Hollywood professionals and the material is reviewed by a Monterey peninsula–based film financier. It offers:

- $2,000 Grand Prize for Best Screenplay
- $1,000 Runner-up Prize
- $1,000 On-location Award

Early entry fee is $40 and is usually due sometime in May. The late fee entry is $50 due by the end of July.
Contact:
Monterey County Film Commission
801 Lighthouse Avenue, Suite 104
Monterey, CA 93940
(831) 646-0910 (telephone); (831) 655-9250 (fax)
info@filmmonterey.org

I helped organize this competition and for months we discussed the rules and regulations that would allow writers a totally fair contest. We left with the conclusion that there was no such thing, but we got about as close as you could get. In order to be completely fair you would have to have the same reader read all the scripts on the same day, at the same time, in the same mood, with no memory of any prior material. Remember, what really counts in these competitions is not just winning, it's getting exposure, because industry professionals read your material.

ACKNOWLEDGMENTS

With many thanks . . .

To Joanne Storkan at Honest Engine Films. I could never ask for a better partner.

To Kevin Falls, for his valuable time and support.

To writers' representative Mitchel Stein, for his professional insights and interviews for both my books.

To Pamela Wallace, for the great experience I've had working with her.

To Chuck Slocum, Assistant Executive Director of the Writers Guild of America, West, for all those helpful statistics.

To my friend and writer Stan Berkowitz, for his interview.

To Gardner Linn, for opening all of our eyes about reality writing.

To Vera Blasi, who continues to amaze me.

To my students, who turned me on to writing again. For their inspiration, the joy, and the great learning experience.

To Jim Long at agoodedit.com, you were terrific.

To Kathy Donnell, for permission to use excerpts of the scripts we wrote during our eight-year partnership. To the good times and the rough times, and to all the work.

To producer Iris Dugow and pros Kathie Fong Yoneda and Michelle Wallerstein, for their insights.

To my editor at Simon & Schuster, Danielle Friedman, who among many talents, has great patience.

To author David Kilpatrick, thanks for your confidence in me.

And, to Barbara Whitworth Taylor, whom I miss terribly. Barbara, if you were still here, this book would have been so much easier and so much more fun.

A very special thanks . . .

To my terrific family, who love and support me.

To my meditation teacher Gurumayi, who keeps chipping away at my stubbornness.

And to my soulmate, Jim Logan, who for sixteen years has been a joy and a great adventure.

INDEX

ABOUT THE AUTHOR

Writer/producer Madeline DiMaggio has sold over forty hours of television and film. Her scripts include prime-time sitcoms, one-hour dramas, TV pilots (both half-hour and one-hour), soaps, animation, Movies-of-the-Week, cable movies, and feature films. Formerly she was writer under contract to Paramount studios in long form and pilot development. She cowrote the feature film *If the Shoe Fits*, starring Rob Lowe and Jennifer Grey, with Pamela Wallace (Academy Award winner for *Witness*). She and Wallace also cowrote the M.O.W. *Alibi*, starring Tori Spelling; the book-to-film feature *Catherine Called Birdy*; and the true-crime screenplay *Murder with Privilege* to Showtime. Currently at Honest Engine Films, DiMaggio produced the feature *Surviving Eden*, starring Peter Dinklage, Jayne Lynch, Sheri Oteri, and Michael Payne, and the documentaries *Stir It Up* and *Humble Beauty*. Honest Engine has numerous projects in development.

Ms. DiMaggio is available for consulting and workshops. Contact her at Cre8asale@aol.com